Praise for *Marketing and Sales Analytics*

"Solid ideas and experiences, well-told, for executives who need higher returns from their analytic investments. Captures many best practices that are consistent with our own experiences at Bain & Company, helping clients develop actionable strategies that deliver sustainable results."

—**Bob Bechek**, Worldwide Managing Director, Bain & Company

"Successful marketing today demands balancing analytic sophistication with the practicality that can put insights to work. Cesar's book synthesizes a set of ideas and case studies that offer proven approaches for getting this balance right."

—**Torrence Boone**, Managing Director of Agency Relations for North America, Google Inc.

"Cesar has explored a complex subject in a clear and useful way as senior marketers look to more effectively leverage the power of data and analytics."

—**Bill Brand**, Chief Marketing and Business Development Officer, HSN, Inc.

"Loaded with meaty lessons from seasoned practitioners, this book defines the guideposts of the Marketing Analytics Age and what it will take for marketing leaders to be successful in it. Cesar Brea has provided a practical playbook for marketers who are ready to make this transition."

—**Meredith Callanan**, Vice President, Corporate Marketing and Communications, T. Rowe Price

"In my time at both Condé Nast and Gilt, we used data extensively to create the best possible experiences for our clients and partners. Cesar's focus on getting the conditions right for analytics, and the experiences he captures to illustrate this theme, bring uniquely valuable perspectives to the conversation on this topic."

—**Sarah Chubb**, Digital Media Consultant, former president, Condé Nast Digital and Gilt City

"*In* Marketing and Sales Analytics, *Cesar Brea takes complex Big Data issues and frames them in a straightforward way that business executives of all kinds will find helpful and enlightening. This book is a great first step to using data analytics strategically to build stronger and more genuine customer relationships that drive growth and profitability.*"

—Chris Malone, Managing Partner, Fidelum Partners and co-author of *The HUMAN Brand: How We Relate to People, Products and Companies*

"*As a provider of a marketing attribution management platform, we work with many leading brands that have charted a course to more holistic measurement across their entire marketing ecosystem. This has resulted in truly actionable insights as well as recommendations for optimizing their overall performance. Cesar's book is a tremendous guide for marketers looking to implement a more integrated, cohesive measurement and optimization strategy, empowered by a data driven approach that's woven into the fabric of their businesses.*

—Manu Mathew, CEO, Visual IQ, Inc.

"*While the field has a lot of books on the statistics of marketing analytics, we also need insights on the organization issues and culture needed to implement successfully. Cesar Brea's* Marketing and Sales Analytics *has addressed this gap in an interesting and helpful way.*"

—Scott A. Neslin, Albert Wesley Frey Professor of Marketing, Tuck School of Business, Dartmouth College

"*Cesar's book comes at a time of unprecedented change for sales and marketing executives. He's captured the transition point between analytics as we have known it with the future of Hadoop and related big data technologies to create a driving force of continuous learning and optimization.*"

—John Schroeder, CEO and Co-founder, MapR Technologies

Marketing and Sales Analytics

Marketing and Sales Analytics

Proven Techniques and Powerful Applications from Industry Leaders

Cesar A. Brea

Associate Publisher: Amy Neidlinger
Executive Editor: Jeanne Glasser Levine
Operations Specialist: Jodi Kemper
Cover Designer: Chuti Prasertsith
Managing Editor: Kristy Hart
Project Editor: Andy Beaster
Copy Editor: Katie Matejka
Proofreader: Jess DeGabriele
Indexer: Cheryl Lenser
Senior Compositor: Nonie Ratcliff
Manufacturing Buyer: Dan Uhrig

Publishing as Pearson
Upper Saddle River, New Jersey 07458

For information about buying this title in bulk quantities, or for special sales opportunities (which may include electronic versions; custom cover designs; and content particular to your business, training goals, marketing focus, or branding interests), please contact our corporate sales department at corpsales@pearsoned.com or (800) 382-3419.

For government sales inquiries, please contact governmentsales@pearsoned.com.

For questions about sales outside the U.S., please contact international@pearsoned.com.

Company and product names mentioned herein are the trademarks or registered trademarks of their respective owners.

First Printing June 2014

ISBN-10: 0-13-359292-8
ISBN-13: 978-0-13-3592924

Pearson Education LTD.
Pearson Education Australia PTY, Limited.
Pearson Education Singapore, Pte. Ltd.
Pearson Education Asia, Ltd.
Pearson Education Canada, Ltd.
Pearson Educación de Mexico, S.A. de C.V.
Pearson Education—Japan
Pearson Education Malaysia, Pte. Ltd.

Library of Congress Control Number: 2014936311

Contents

Foreword

Cesar's book has arrived at an exciting moment. Thanks to the unprecedented amount of data that businesses now have at their fingertips, smart analytics can help shape marketing and sales like never before. With social networks, loyalty programs, mobile apps and all kinds of data-rich technologies providing new insights into peoples' likes, dislikes, behaviors and interests, brands can go beyond simple demographics and engage with consumers at a level previously not possible. Consider, for example, how retailers use analytics to personalize every customer touch point, whether it's an email, ad, or live interaction with a salesperson at the register—and how brands are using data to personalize not just messages, but also the experiences they deliver to their customers. We truly are breaking new ground in terms of how much more relevant and powerful our strategies can become.

With these increasing opportunities for engagement in mind, how can today's businesses set the stage for analytic success? This book, which synthesizes Cesar's experience from a long, varied career spanning marketing, sales, and technology—as well as insights and lessons learned from more than a dozen accomplished executives—provides a solid template for planning your analytics evolution.

Beyond focusing on internal tools and the analysts that use them, Cesar outlines the importance of cultivating a broader set of resources, capabilities, and even attitudes. He helps readers solidify a clear vision for engaging analytics, and provides practical advice about how to build a roadmap for moving forward. And, since I've known Cesar for nearly 25 years in a variety of professional capacities, it's no surprise that he presents these ideas not only skillfully, but also in his typical straightforward, approachable way. More than just theory, he delivers nuts and bolts analytic strategies that readers can deploy immediately.

During the course of my own long career in advertising, marketing, and technology, I've been a proponent of the use of innovative technologies to shape, plan, execute, measure, and refine media and creative strategies. Analytics are a critical part of this. For example, data optimization is the driving force behind programmatic technologies designed to automate processes for advertisers, agencies and publishers, which are rapidly changing how an increasing volume of digital inventory is bought and sold. Sophisticated algorithms spin data into valuable insight, empowering every brand—no matter how big or small—to continually test, learn about, and optimize their campaign planning. All of this is done in order to consistently deliver the most compelling message, at the right time, on the right screen and devices, to the right consumer. The coming together of technology, media and creative is what I like to call *convergence*. Brands that are able to effectively align these three disciplines, while also taking advantage of all the insights that analytics have to offer, will realize the most powerful results.

This book will help your business build a more thoughtful, converged, and well-executed marketing and sales analytics strategy, which is vital in today's data-driven world. Knowledgeable, curious, and technically savvy, Cesar is an excellent guide for readers who are ready to take their analytics approach to the next level.

—**Bob Lord**
Chief Executive Officer, AOL Platforms

Acknowledgments

Even in the world of analytics, where "what you know" would seem to be what it's all about, "who you know" still comes up trumps. At least that's what I discovered in writing this book, as regardless of how much direct experience or book learning I amassed, it would not have been remotely possible without the generosity of clients, friends, colleagues, and mentors from across the years.

First, of course, I'd like to thank the executives I interviewed for their enthusiasm for the project and their patience with my many questions. For me, the best part of this book is hearing their stories and perspectives directly, and hopefully I haven't mangled things too badly in the attempt to illustrate some main ideas with their perspectives. It was truly an honor to spend time with each of them, and I'll be a better professional for it.

Next, I'd like to thank friends who were especially generous in making introductions that led to these conversations as well as suggestions for the book, and in particular to Tip Clifton, Mark deCollibus, Joe Fuller, Perry Hewitt, Judy Honig, Blaise Heltai, Jeffrey Hupe, Bob Lord, and Erica Seidel. I'm also grateful to friends, colleagues, and mentors whose experiences and relationships in this field I've learned and benefitted from, including Mike Bernstein, Lee Bissonnette, Susan Ellerin, Sheldon Gilbert, Trish Gorman, Ben Kline, Janelle Leonard, Jay Leonard, Bob Neuhaus, Jeffrey Rayport, Tad Staley, and my business partner Jamie Schein. Special thanks go to Judah Phillips for introducing me to Jeanne Glasser Levine, my editor at Pearson, and to Jeanne and her colleagues for their guidance and support through this project. Your confidence in me was inspiring and I hope the result justifies your faith!

I'm grateful also to the clients who, daily, give my colleagues and me the opportunities to work with and learn from them. This is an arena where the clay is still very wet, and there's no substitute (not even this book!) for the time spent with them.

Finally, I'd like to thank my wife Nan and my children, Ben, Kate, and Will, who bore the brunt of this effort through a tough winter, and who now face the prospect of more fun in Phase Two of The Master Plan (which I'll reveal as soon as I figure one out). The answer to "Where did you find the time?" lies with them.

About the Author

Cesar A. Brea is Managing Partner of Force Five Partners, LLC (forcefivepartners.com), a marketing analytics agency that works with clients in a number of industries to design and execute multi-channel marketing and sales strategies, and to build pragmatic, sustainable analytic foundations.

Cesar has more than twenty years experience as a line executive, advisor, and entrepreneur. Prior to co-founding Force Five Partners in 2008, Cesar served as Global Practice Leader for Marketspace, the digital media and marketing practice of Monitor Group, the international strategy consulting firm founded by Harvard Business School Professor Michael Porter. Formerly, Cesar was CEO of Contact Networks, an early LinkedIn competitor sold to Thomson Financial in 2006, and was Senior Vice President for Sales and Marketing at Razorfish, the world's leading digital advertising agency. Before Razorfish, Cesar was Vice President for Marketing and Business Development at ArsDigita Corporation, an open-source software firm focused on online communities acquired by Red Hat Software in 2002. Earlier, Cesar was a management consultant at Bain & Company and a banker at J.P. Morgan.

Cesar holds an MBA from Dartmouth's Amos Tuck School, where he was named an Edward Tuck Scholar, and received his undergraduate degree from Harvard College. He is a frequent writer and speaker on marketing in the digital age. In 2012, Cesar published his first book on this topic, *Pragmalytics: Practical Approaches to Marketing Analytics in the Digital Age*. Cesar has been a guest lecturer in undergraduate and graduate programs at MIT and Harvard, and writes about marketing and ebusiness on his blog at http://octavianworld.org, and on Twitter (@cesarbrea).

Cesar and his wife Nan Leonard live in Dover, Massachusetts, and have three children, Ben, Kate, and Will. On summer weekends, they enjoy sailing on Nantucket Sound.

Introduction

This is a book of, by, and for senior executives who want to build marketing and sales analytics capabilities that will produce significant competitive advantages for their firms.

The core idea of this book is that successful marketing and sales analytics is much more about creating and sustaining conditions for success than it is about the brilliance of any particular insight.

When you are done reading this book, you will:

- Be able to assess and enhance important eco-systemic conditions crucial to the success of your analytic investments and efforts

- Have a simple, practical set of frameworks, techniques, and guidance you can use to organize, manage, communicate and, govern your analytic efforts for maximum impact

- Have a range of real-world experiences and lessons from accomplished executives that will give you both some specific ideas to pursue and general lessons to apply

Why This Book

Last September, at an analytics conference in Berkeley, I was having breakfast with Mohammed "Mo" Chaara, a director in Lenovo's corporate analytics group. He asked a good question: "With all the potential value to be realized from Big Data in so many domains, why has it evolved more quickly in the world of sales and marketing? Why not, for example, in delivering health care, a much more important challenge where much more money is spent?" That was kind of deep for seven-thirty in the morning, before the first cup of coffee. But "Pride goeth..." so I waded in anyway. "Here are three ideas. First, maybe because the technologies that generate digital data have seen their first main expression as enablers of a new communication medium, and sales and marketing are prime use cases for this medium. Second, because there are large and clearly defined budgets for the old media, which the new medium competes with in a much more accountable way. And third, sales and marketing are, relatively speaking, less constrained by regulation—nobody dies if a display ad is mistargeted." Mo nodded patiently and politely. We munched on our toast quietly, and the conversation shifted to something else.

Whether or not you like my answer to Mo's question, in the world(s) of sales and marketing, this is indisputably the Age of Analytics. Pundit after pundit, in book and article and talk upon book and article and talk, bows before the Big Data *zeitgeist*. And we don't just have abstract prophecies, but also accessible avatars to reinforce this reality. In the vanguard of the modern economy, a small group of firms—the major digital advertising networks, for example—provide not only revolutionary services to their users, value to their customers, and returns to their investors today, but also fully-realized, continuously-evolving visions of what the data-driven future holds.

The Rest Of Us follow, in a modern-day migration that makes prior evolutions of these functional areas look quaint. There are other success stories, of course, but for virtually all, the journey is hard and full of obstacles; our collective results confirm this. If just a few months ago we spoke of "data lakes," some now speak of "data landfills."[1] Last August, the physicist-turned-journalist James Glanz had a piece in *The New York Times* titled, "Is Big Data An Economic Dud?" The article, and others like it at the time, marked an inflection point in the usual hype cycle that surrounds things like this. Glanz noted that despite all the data now available, along with ever-more powerful tools to exploit it, "There is just one tiny problem: the economy is, at best, in the doldrums and has stayed there during the latest surge in web traffic."[2] Other research echoes his observation, with numbers. For example, a study by *Wikibon* founder and researcher Jeffrey F. Kelley published in September 2013, spanning 100 firms implementing Big Data capabilities, found an average ROI of just 55 cents on every dollar invested and noted "a lack of compelling business use case" among three main causes.[3]

"Be patient," you might say, "It's just a matter of time." Of course you'd be right, and I'd agree. (Sadly) programmed as I am, some of the usual-suspect business frameworks, like Gartner Group's Hype Cycle[4], sprang to my mind to frame his piece. But other voices crowded in too. I thought of the futurist Roy Amara's saying, "We tend to overestimate the effect of a technology in the short run and underestimate the effect in the long run."[5] The science fiction

---

[1] Roberts, Jeff John, "When data lakes become landfills: how to avoid drowning in surplus information," *Gigaom.com*, September 9, 2013, http://gigaom.com/2013/09/19/when-data-lakes-become-landfills-how-to-avoid-drowning-in-surplus-information/.

[2] Glanz, James, "Is Big Data an Economic Big Dud?," *nytimes.com*, August 17, 2013, http://www.nytimes.com/2013/08/18/sunday-review/is-big-data-an-economic-big-dud.html.

[3] Kelly, Jeff, "Enterprises Struggling to Derive Maximum Value from Big Data," *Wikibon.org*, September 19, 2013, http://wikibon.org/wiki/v/Enterprises_Struggling_to_Derive_Maximum_Value_from_Big_Data.

[4] "Research Methodologies," Gartner, http://www.gartner.com/technology/research/methodologies/hype-cycle.jsp.

[5] "Roy Amara," http://en.wikipedia.org/wiki/Roy_Amara.

novelist William Gibson flashed to me: "The future's already here—it's just not very evenly distributed."[6] Finally, I remembered Arthur C. Clarke, maybe interpreting Gandhi for the corporate crowd: "New ideas pass through three periods: 1) It can't be done. 2) It probably can be done, but it's not worth doing. 3) I knew it was a good idea all along!"[7]

These are wonderful aphorisms, but they are not Manifest Destiny. The order in which organizations come to the promised future matters a great deal. Pioneers may get killed, but settlers get very, very rich, and once new data-driven industry structures form, it gets very hard to buck their economic realities. So, starting six years ago, rather than starting yet another tool vendor and joining the "supply-side" evangelical bandwagon, I've been much more interested in working on the "demand side," helping large organizations that face complex, multi-channel sales and marketing investment and execution challenges, to accelerate the pace at which they realize the potential those frameworks and sayings suggest.

To bundle up what I thought I had learned, I wrote a short book a couple of years ago titled *Pragmalytics: Practical Approaches to Marketing in the Digital Age*, which summarizes experiences and insights that were useful to me in my work. *Pragmalytics* explores three ideas. First, successful marketing and sales analytics are mostly *not* about whether My Algorithm Can Beat Up Your Algorithm, but are instead about cultivating what I've called "Eco-systemic Conditions." Second, planning backwards from desired business results, and not forward from the allure of a concept, keeps you both focused on bottlenecks for getting to results and disciplined about how much to invest in opening each bottleneck before moving on to the next constraint. Third, informed partly by things I've been exposed to in

---

[6] "William Gibson," http://en.wikipedia.org/wiki/William_Gibson.

[7] "Arthur C. Clarke Quotes," *Brainyquote.com*, http://www.brainyquote.com/quotes/authors/a/arthur_c_clarke.html.

other aspects of my life, is the idea of applying behavioral science lessons to address change management challenges that the analytics revolution demands.

However, hearing about those experiences through my filters isn't as interesting and useful as it would be to hear directly from a range of senior executives who have had to build their firms' sales and marketing analytics capabilities in real time while also driving business results under the tumultuous conditions of recent years; they are the people who have been changing the tires at seventy miles an hour. So while my earlier synthesis suggests a structure to organize around and some hypotheses to pressure test, the main reason for this book is to enrich the how-to gene pool with some executive-level bio-diversity. I hope you'll agree it's a vast improvement.

Who It's For

By now, an effective analytic capability supporting marketing and sales is not just something your board, or your boss, suggest *might* be worthwhile to explore—it's something they demand. The competitive examples of organizations doing this are out there and well documented. Inside your own shop, forecasts are expected to be tighter and less subjective. And in today's highly digital world, operations are expected to be driven, increasingly automatically and close to real time, by these predictions.

In response, you've hired the staff or outsourced the work to your agency/systems integrator/consultant. You've bought (or you're renting) the tools, and your teams have done first or second generations of analytic work. But the sheen of the first six months to "implement the capability," capped often with cool visualizations describing insights with potential value, has dulled. Now, you're under pressure to show some business results for your investments and efforts, and you can't do it alone. You've got to pull people together, coordinate them, and even, when necessary, show them how.

So, you are one of four people.

1. You are the top functional (marketing and/or sales) executive, responsible for getting leverage from the analytic capability you're investing in—you need to show results on key business metrics.

2. You are the top analytic executive, charged with building and managing the resources that generate insights and communicates and packages them in a way that they can be acted on appropriately.

3. You are a student, in an academic setting or business training program, that not only seeks to produce technical competence but functional awareness—the difference between, for example, how to throw a forward pass and how to lead your team down the field to score.

4. You are a teacher in such a program, seeking to illustrate and enrich what can be dry topics with a sense for how they will be applied in practice.

Where It Fits

If you're reading into this field, you may have observed three kinds of writing. At the highest level (where level means perspective, not just quality), primarily for the C-suite and aspirants thereto, there are "evangelistic" titles, like Tom Davenport's *Competing On Analytics* and Ian Ayres' *Supercrunchers*. These works do a good job of calling attention to, describing, and illustrating the Big Data *zeitgeist*.

At the coalface of the data mines there are "how-to" guides for the analyst and the first-line manager charged with supporting decision-makers. Avinash Kaushik's excellent *Web Analytics: An Hour A Day* and its successors are some of my favorites; another wonderful effort is *Visualize This* by Nathan Yau. Even Edward Tufte's classics, such as *The Visual Display of Quantitative Information*, fall into this category for me.

In the middle are books aimed more at managers and executives who have to define questions worth asking and then orchestrate resources not just to answer them, but also to act on them. The best example of this very practical guide approach I've read recently is Judah Phillips' *Building A Digital Analytics Organization* (Pearson, 2013).[8] (Judah kindly agreed to be interviewed for this book, and— full disclosure—also generously introduced me to my editor Jeanne Glasser Levine and her colleagues at Pearson.) My book fits into this middle tier. It differs from Phillips' book by coming at the analytics challenge more from the requirements end and by offering the reader a chance to interpolate where he or she may end up through hearing a variety of practitioner perspectives. In this sense, the two books are highly complementary.

How to Use It

I hope you'll use this book in two ways. First, it can help you organize your thinking about how to tackle an analytically intensive initiative. Think of the specific suggestions here as "scaffolding" checklists for how to shape a question, or anticipate and address some challenges to it. Second, I hope it will provide you with experiences from other executives that help you calibrate your current situation and approach, or assess where you should be. The examples here are certainly not exhaustive, or even "statistically significant" for representing

---

[8] Phillips, Judah, *Building A Digital Analytics Organization*, (Pearson, 2013), http://www.amazon.com/Building-Digital-Analytics-Organization-Integrating/dp/0133372782.

the full range of challenges you might face, but they do have enough in common (and are sufficiently different) that they can help give you and others you need to influence a sense for your own needs and potential ways forward.

A word about focus: In the context of Professor Jerome McCarthy's "4Ps of Marketing" framework (Product, Price, Place-ment, and Promotion)[9], my judgment is that most of the action today that's driving the evolution of marketing and sales analytics is in the "Placement" dimension—in particular, the rapid evolution of native digital channels like mobile device advertising and the digitization of legacy channels like print. So, there's a disproportionate amount of attention to these elements of the marketing mix here.

How It's Organized

The book has four parts.

Part I, "Improving Your Odds: Eco-systemic Conditions for Ana-lytic Success," explores what I call "eco-systemic conditions." These include strategic alignment (agreeing on opportunities worth inves-tigating), access to data, operational flexibility (being able, through a combination of infrastructure, process, and people readiness, to act on insights generated through analytics), and individual and organi-zational capacity. We start here because a recurring theme across all the experiences described in this book as well as my own is that with-out getting these conditions right, investments you make in analytic capabilities will not generate returns. It's like buying a prize-winning pumpkin seed and trying to grow it on a parking lot's blacktop.

Part II, "Practical Analytics: Proven Techniques and Heuris-tics," explores how practitioners apply research, analytic, and testing

---

[9] McCarthy, Jerome E., *Basic Marketing. A Managerial Approach,* (1960), Home-wood, IL: Richard D. Irwin.

techniques and heuristics in real-world situations to strike a balance between thoroughness and practicality as they seek to inform decisions and actions. Included in this section is a discussion of the value and limitations of stories, and more generally hypotheses, to guide analytic approaches in this time. Also, we'll explore specific techniques for managing bias in "uncontrolled" decision-making settings.

Part III, "Making Progress," conceives of analytic capabilities as living, breathing things that need to make continuous, carefully throttled progress to stay vital and provide feedback, and it suggests how to evolve these capabilities. So, it explores the balance between building these capabilities and delivering insights and supporting actions through those capabilities. In particular, it explores issues of pace, governance, and measurement of the productivity of analytic capabilities themselves.

Finally, Part IV, "Conversations with Practitioners," presents summaries of the conversations I had with the executives who agreed to participate in this project. Of course, relevant aspects of these conversations are woven throughout the first three parts to help illustrate and extend the ideas presented there, but I found it equally valuable to take in their perspectives as they conveyed them. Sometimes these were presented in the context of their firms' recent histories; other times they came in musings on specific technical topics; and some came through in the narrative arc of career stories. For me, they were all fascinating and useful, and I'm sure you'll feel the same way.

Any book on a subject that's evolving this quickly can only hope to be a temporary push on a carousel of progress. Ongoing conversations among operators and analysts in the arena are the real fuel for learning, and I hope I'll have the chance to talk with you. So if you have comments or questions about the ideas here, I'm @cesarbrea on Twitter or please email me at cbrea@forcefivepartners.com.

Part I
Improving Your Odds: Eco-systemic Conditions for Analytic Success

Ecosystemic Conditions for Analytic Success

	Weak	Moderate	Strong
Strategic Alignment	"Haven't discussed misaligned objectives—each group submits separate plans, is handed separate budget, executes against different metrics."	"Have considered aligning objectives—discussing in context of managing 'customer experience' or 'multi-channel campaign' (for example)—but haven't resolved."	"Clear articulation of and prioritization among different objectives."
Access To Data	Undocumented architecture and access, Inflexible reporting.	Documented architecture and data elements, but access logistically complex and expensive. Reporting of financial results via BI tools, but limited access to those.	Documented, pre-staged (warehouse or ready access). Dashboards, visualization and modeling tools in use.
Operational Flexibility	Limited / highly manual / un-integrated marketing platforms.	Has marketing automation platform (e.g., Marketo, Unica) but limited use of capabilities for cross-channel, highly-targeted programs. Limited integration.	Extensive testing / personalization capabilities and experience, efficient provisioning of creative for executions. Consistent, well-governed integration.
Analytic Marketer Capability	Silo-ed approach to marketing, including management of multiple agency partners. Limited experience with data-driven decision-making. Significant emphasis on primary research (focus groups, etc.). Skepticism about / resistance to attribution analysis (beyond champion). Significant education and incentives review required.	Ad hoc collaboration among marketing functions, but limited process / governance for coordinating efforts. Some experience with attribution, even if heuristic. Episodic media mix models. Open-minded about attribution, but resource-or experience-constrained (or both).	Firm governance process for working with agencies. Significant familiarity / facility with digital data and model-driven marketing among team members. Culture of continuous analysis, testing, learning.

Figure 1.1   Eco-systemic Conditions for Analytic Success

1

Strategic Alignment—First You Need to Agree On What to Ask

Any number of articles and books about "data science" (side note: the term's a bit oxymoronic, I think) emphasize the importance of asking the right question. "If I had an hour to solve a problem, I'd spend 55 minutes thinking about the problem and five minutes thinking about solutions," said Albert Einstein famously.[1] Personally, while I'd want to get a peek at the data I had to work with a little before the 55th minute of the hour to see how close it might get me to answering the questions I'd really like to pursue, his point is well-taken. In the context of marketing and sales analytics, as elsewhere, the ultimate questions are where to shift scarce resources like dollars and people.

Most books on analytics start with a list of common questions and techniques for how to solve them. This book starts differently, by trying to understand the decision-makers who must absorb and act on your analysis. One important realization our real-world questions suggest is that the ultimate resource-related questions we describe above are rarely asked and answered by a single individual alone.

People have different ways of defining possible challenges to focus on, ways of evaluating performance, and means for assessing tradeoffs among possible solutions to challenges. So, for any decision-making

---

[1] Although this quote, or variants of it, is widely attributed to Einstein, the date and place where he said this remain enigmatic. For more, see http://en.wikiquote.org/wiki/Talk:Albert_Einstein

process with more than one participant, Einstein's advice should be extended to weaving these three elements into a *deliberation structure* that each person with a hand in the decision can connect to, even as you try to select an *analytic structure* most suited to the business challenge or opportunity at hand. If you can't get senior executives who will use the fruits of the analytic labor to agree on what they want, or even how to ask for it, you are doomed.

In this chapter, we'll explore how different executives think about these needs and suggest a synthesis that might serve as a point of departure for you. We'll also highlight some common organizational "fault lines" that you'll have to navigate and offer some ideas for how to recognize and address them. Then, in Part II, "Practical Analytics: Proven Techniques and Heuristics," we'll present analytic frameworks and techniques that can serve as candidate "common currencies" for facilitating strategic alignment across the divides we identify in this chapter.

Framing Your Focus Beyond the Answer Itself

So, first, there's the question of where to focus your analytic attention. My former boss George Bennett, who co-founded Bain & Company and then successfully built and sold several services firms after that, used to say, "Come prepared to talk; be prepared to listen." Consistent with his advice, the first challenge is to develop your own perspectives on possible questions and answers from multiple angles, not only for a richer set of options, but also to help you identify and compensate for your own biases. At the same time, you need to understand what questions others are asking and what solution options they might be lobbying for, as well as what logic and fact set led them to their conclusions. Then, while you can't satisfy everyone all the time, you can provide discipline as to how priorities get set that goes beyond the individual analyses you've done. If people feel that the processes for deciding where and how to spend scarce resources are rigorous and fair, they'll be better able to accept the answers. In our conversations for this book, Judah Phillips (who has built and run the digital analytics functions at Monster.com and elsewhere, and has written an excellent book on the subject called *Building The Digital Analytics Organization*) memorably suggested, "If information is power, then analytics is inevitably a political act," and you have to think several moves ahead about how to influence direction and progress in the best interests of the business. (We'll tackle this third issue more extensively in Part III, "Making Progress.")

Three Perspectives for Marketing and Sales Analytics

The conversations for this book suggest three main orientations executives have for marketing and sales analytics. For short, I call them "Venus," "Mars," and "Earth." "Venus" is primarily a way to tell "outside-in" customer experience stories about how people connect to your firm, and how your sales and marketing efforts map and execute against the contexts these customer experiences define. By contrast, "Mars" is an "inside-out" numbers-first way of thinking about how you should shift marketing investments across different channels. Today, "Attribution Analysis" (the Big Data Brother of media mix modeling) is the most well known specific technique for this angle on marketing thinking. Finally, "Earth" describes an "infrastructure-up" order for building properties and presences that is essentially reasoned from a blank slate ("Ok, first we need a web site, then we need a mobile version of it, then we need to be on Twitter..."). The sequence the Earth perspective suggests is generically sensible, but typically untethered from an appraisal of how your specific customers want to navigate toward purchases and of the relative performance of your current investments to help them.

Different senior executives have, through their backgrounds and inclinations, a dominant framework among these three that influences them. Creatives like to tell stories. Analysts like to talk numbers (and with the glorification of quants on Wall Street, marketing analysts now also talk in terms of "arbitrages" and "trades" as well). Builders express themselves in terms of "foundational capabilities" with "end-state" visions, phased plans, and "process designs" for managing them. Because of these biases, senior teams with similar backgrounds run the risk of groupthink and missed opportunities, while other teams with widely differing backgrounds run the risk of confusion and paralysis. So in addition to the intrinsic value each framework offers on its own, using them collectively is very helpful so team members can tune into each other's points of view.

Venus

Various analytic disciplines apply the same fundamental Venus perspective using different terms. Strategists talk about "customer segments," the "pathways" each customer travels, through a grid defined by "buying process" stages on one axis and "channels" on the other. Business (or "functional") analysts talk in terms of "users" and "use cases," also frequently documented using process maps or requirements documents for technical solutions. Creatives talk in terms of "personas," "occasions," and "touchpoints," bundled into "narratives." Regardless, Venusians like stories, and so the common denominator for them, regardless of functional training and experience, is the largely "left-to-right" narrative arc of the "customer experience."

If numbers are introduced into the resulting Venusian stories, they are expressed as costs-per-something (for example, per impression, click, lead, or acquisition) at each step, or as a percentage yield from one step to the next (for example, conversion rate). But very often they are not included at all—a crucial miss. Even more rarely are they updated. A more common outcome is a beautiful flowchart, capturing the existing or desired experience in amber, displayed in a large framed print on an office wall.

Mars

Martians like data. So they take what various channels produce and look for significant answers to the question, "When I change x (and y and z), what happens to a (and b and c)." Then they divide costs by these results working toward the holy grail—a common currency for "pricing" investments for different options ("full attribution"). Next, they use these "prices" to "buy" and "sell" media, messages, and audiences (at the extreme, this could be in real time, such as real-time bidding in display ad markets).

Today, there's lots of data. And, the relationship among different data is increasingly *deterministic* (I see search result X and click through to page Y) rather than *probabilistic* (I see BigCo's TV ad X, and later visit BigCo's store Y). Further, the tools for capturing and making sense of all this (cloud computing, Hadoop and its friends, modeling and visualization packages, and so on) are widely available and more cost effective than anything to this point.

On the other hand, data volumes can be overwhelming, the data itself can be very messy and hard to integrate, and with so many moving parts, analyzing and acting on it can be pretty complex. Skills to set up, use, and interpret the available and affordable tools are scarce. Plus, there's the classic joke: "Q: Why does the drunk man look for his lost keys under the lamp post, instead of the bushes where he fell? A: Because that's where the light is!" In other words, by starting with data we *do* have about the things we *are* doing for the people we *do* see, we miss opportunities to do things we don't yet do, for people we don't yet know.

Among the three perspectives, Martians are the most likely to test as well. Because of their primary orientation to data and not to design, they don't fall in love with their creations and confuse these means for ends. On the other hand, their relatively lower engagement with design of infrastructures and experiences sometimes limits their orientation to data-rich and test-friendly channels, recapitulating the "drunken man" dynamic described above. Smart executives see this bias, and while they respect and embrace the discipline of an analytic, test-oriented mindset, they don't allow it to dominate their options. Speaking of La-Z-Boy's analytically-inclined culture, CMO Doug Collier says, "It's almost a joke...'If you don't bring me a control group, don't bother talking to me!'" He explains the firm's insistence on a "double-delta": "Don't just tell me how we compare with past performance—I also need to understand the lift over control." So now, "Even the PR and brand guys will come in with numbers to support their suggestions." Yet at the same time, speaking of the firm's significant investment in its brand awareness campaign through a relationship with the actress and model Brooke Shields, "Signing Brooke wasn't something you could do as a test. We had to go, and we felt combining Brooke's appeal with our prior brand equity would lead our target customers to give us a chance." However, speaking to the data-driven discipline balance he tries to strike, he added, "On the other hand, we didn't just jump; we did a lot of careful qualitative and quantitative research on our brand platform to shape our advertising. We didn't want to make Brooke the brand, but rather have her be the vehicle through which our target customers could discover that our product line fits their lifestyle, and that our stores are great places to shop." The firm has done seventeen spots with Ms. Shields so far, and has the analytic infrastructure in place (including the use of extensive quantitative and qualitative testing of the spots in primary research, and the YouGov *BrandIndex* service extended with some custom questions focused on the awareness and effect of the brand platform) to understand, scientifically, which spots, in what combinations, are effectively conveying which messages at different times.

Earth

People of Earth are more architects and engineers than operators. In the absence of good Venusian stories and Martian models to guide their paths, they document the "current state," envision an "end state," and then plot and launch phased programs for getting from A to B. But if you look more closely, very often the starting and ending points are described more in terms of capability inputs than performance outputs and milestones for deciding when what you've built is good enough and it's time to move to the next part of your plan. Or, if implementation of capabilities is tied to related operating metrics and not just schedules, it's sometimes hard to make investment trade-offs without the kind of common currency that Martians might prefer.[2]

The "builder bias"—the tendency to use this lens—is especially prevalent in digital marketing, because many of the senior people in this domain came up at a time when their priority was to field basic capabilities, rather than optimize pre-existing ones. Rob Schmults, VP of Online Commerce at Talbots, says:

> If you asked a physical store manager, "How's business?" you'd never hear, "Well, this month we installed new lighting, and the talking price tags go live next month." They'd be less about pixels, and more about stockout rates in popular sizes. By contrast, ask an ecommerce person, "What's on deck for next year?" and he or she tends to focus on "Design and

---

[2] One excellent example of this approach is a blog post by Google Digital Marketing Evangelist and Market Motive (http://www.marketmotive.com/) co-founder Avinash Kaushik, titled "Digital Marketing and Analytics: Two Ladders for Magnificent Success," in which he suggests an *ur*-sequence for digital marketing initiatives and the metrics to go with them. (http://www.kaushik.net/avinash/digital-marketing-analytics-ladder-step-by-step-success/)

launch site x or feature y" and relatively less on the performance of what they are operating. This means time and time
again you see insufficient attention given to inventory levels,
to basic usability and shopability. A physical store manager
is going to raise bloody murder if she's hollowed out on core
sizes in core product. She's also going to be absolutely certain
her store is easy to get around. The online counterpart all too
often gets distracted by shiny keys.

At minimum, even with weak ties to operating metrics such as
feedback loops, one thing our executives suggested looking for, to
distinguish more- and less-effective applications of the "Earth" perspective, is how iterative these applications are. In other words, ideally they try to keep implementation progress in balance across your
"experience": make a little progress on the website, then shift to promotion, then back to your mobile site, then perhaps some attention
to social media presence, and so on. This requires, of course, some
coordinating mechanism and a strong team culture in which senior
folks responsible for different pieces know when to "lead, follow, or
get out of the way."

Applying the Three Approaches

All three of these ways of looking at the world are enormously
enabling and yet limiting at the same time. In our discussions, our
executives don't see using them as "either-or" but rather, "What mix,
and when?" Here are some guidelines synthesized from their advice:

---

[3] Jeremy Hsu, "The Secrets of Good Storytelling: Why We Love a Good Yarn,"
Scientific American, August-September, 2008, http://www.scientificamerican.
com/article.cfm?id=the-secrets-of-storytelling.

- When you can't get on the same page, lead with Venus. Research shows that humans are wired for stories[3], so the Venusian approach is the most effective common denominator for driving the strategic alignment process in a heterogeneous senior team. But don't forget the numbers: Quantitatively expressed facts about yields and costs can then be layered into the stories to provide proportion and help you generalize the points your narratives make.

- When you need to maximize your near-term ROI and have limited degrees of freedom to build new stuff, emphasize Mars. Move pragmatically but persistently toward the fully-attributed future by adding more variables, source by source, to your analysis. Prioritize each successive addition by the magnitude of your spending and your flexibility to act. (It may, for example, be easier to tweak your promotional strategy, or your digital spending, than to redo your TV campaign.) Wring as much result from your existing spending through shrewd "trading" so you have more to reinvest in the re-imagined future.

- When you need to accelerate progress, be an Earthling. Don't over-think, look for obvious improvements you can make quickly, and focus on stringing together a series of these successes to get the ball rolling. Momentum is strategic, too. But make sure as you do these things that you don't just measure your progress in lines of code, but in their impact on key operating metrics (like the ones Avinash Kaushik described)—and watch for diminishing returns to tell you when to shift gears.

Figure 1.2 summarizes the perspectives and when to apply them. Even as you emphasize one approach for a particular set of circumstances, keep pilot lights lit under the others. It won't just help you get better answers—it will also make folks with different inclinations feel heard, which is just as (or more) important.

Analytic Orientation

	"Venus"	"Mars"	"Earth"
Personality/Background	Creative	Trader	Engineer
Thinks in terms of...	Customer Experience	Optimization	Architecture
Communicates with...	Stories	Numbers	Plans
Go-to artifact	"Customer Journey"	Predictive Model	Blueprint
Most useful when...	You need initial alignment among members of a senior team.	You need short term ROI improvement and have limited ability to build new channels.	You are operating in a new market and need to accelerate progress or experiment to find your way forward.

Figure 1.2   Analytic Orientation

Reconciling Organizational and Cultural Perspectives

If only it were as simple as reconciling Venus, Mars, and Earth! In addition to the "intrinsic" mindsets or approaches different people carry, there are also "extrinsic" fault lines to consider. These are extrinsic in the sense that they are a function of organizational constructs, related interests, and "tribal" dynamics, more than native personality traits and experiences of individual executives. These divisions exist to varying degrees in all organizations, and you ignore them at your peril. In what could well be a corollary to Einstein's proposition about the importance of asking the right question, there's Peter Drucker's famous observation that "Culture eats strategy for breakfast."[4]

Across our conversations, the executives interviewed for this book called out eight fault lines they've experienced to be relevant. Listed below and in Figure 1.3, six are functionally defined, and two are more a matter of culture.

---

[4] This remark is widely attributed to Professor Drucker, but does not appear in his writings or records of his speeches.

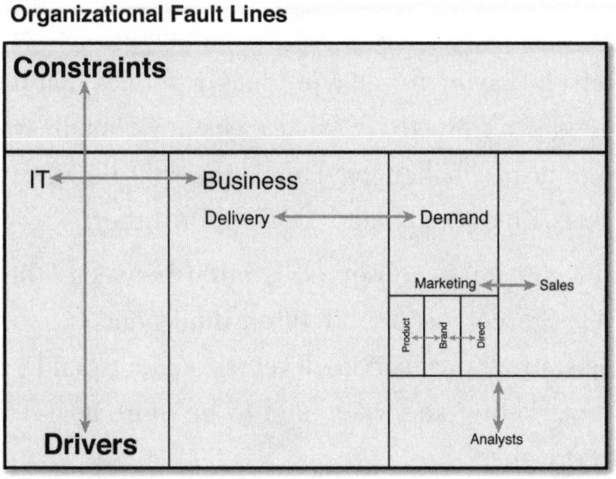

Organizational Fault Lines

Figure 1.3   Organizational Fault Lines

1. One major border lies between marketing and sales, demarcated by the Qualified Lead. This is a hotly disputed division everywhere, even in film: recall the famous scene in "Glengarry Glen Ross" where Alec Baldwin dresses down the sales team after they complain about the quality of the leads they have to work with.[5]

2. Inside the marketing function, we often find a split between brand, product, and direct marketers, who, variously, come from "creative," "strategic," and "analytic" backgrounds.

3. It's common also to find a split between analytical or research teams on one side, and the "line" sales and marketing executives they serve; this is especially true when analytical resources are collected together someplace and segregated, physically and organizationally from their "customers." The supposed advantages of "critical mass" then have to be actively cultivated, through training, sharing, and cross-disciplinary collaboration, to offset the costs of isolation that are charged by default.

---

[5] Movieclips.com, "Put That Coffee Down!" excerpted from *Glengarry Glen Ross* by David Mamet http://www.youtube.com/watch?v=r6Lf8GtMe4M.

4. There's often a strong "demand" vs. "delivery" animus. Having to make, serve, or support what someone else promises, or, conversely, having to sell a product or service that inevitably as designed can't exactly fit what a customer might want to buy, are significant challenges. Hence the split between marketing and sales, on one side, and "ops" on the other.

5. The biggest chasm observed is often between "the business" and IT. Stereotypically, IT often thinks and talks in terms of projects, programs, service level agreements, and governance, while marketing and sales tend to be more goal-oriented and quota-driven.

6. The "driver" functions—marketing, sales, IT, operations—also eternally struggle with "constraint" functions, such as finance, legal, and even HR.

7. There's the classic "home office vs. the field" tension, best expressed by the cynical saying, "Hi, we're from corporate, and we're here to help!"

8. Finally, there's a natural tension that emerges between "old-culture insiders" and "new-culture outsiders" when an acquisition is completed or a senior executive is hired and slowly works to bring in "his or her own people." The lines of demarcation here are often stylistic, even when functional, experiential, or educational backgrounds are similar. Examples of these stylistic lines include patience versus urgency, consensual versus autocratic, degrees of polish and formality, and politeness versus directness, among many others.

How you select and mix frameworks, and how you communicate the insights they lead to, must also start with a careful appraisal of the relative importance of, and degree of stress on, each of these fault lines. At one level, what questions to ask may seem obvious ("How do we increase sales and profits?"). But depending on your training and experience, your role, your incentives, and your particular pressures, your interests and needs can run in a very different direction from your senior peers'. Each of the groups described above will have its own idea of what questions should be asked and its own frameworks for determining those questions. For example:

- Salespeople will want clear qualification criteria with solid data.
- Finance people will want logical, well-founded (benchmarks and past precedents) business cases.
- IT people will want explicit requirements, prioritization, and timing.
- Field people will want useful, high quality "templates" (both specific and conceptual) that leave room for them to innovate, along with data for which template works best.

If you can't get some agreement on what to pursue, your investment in analytic capability building isn't likely to pay off. If you're not careful to balance the language you use across different groups' dialects, or to find some plainspoken common denominator, you will miss people. Also, you must be sensitive and intentional to perceived allocations of credit (or blame) when you present certain facts. For example, is a low or inefficient conversion from one step to the next the fault of the quality of the lead or the skill of the closer? Decisions about where to focus your de-averaging and modeling efforts will be guided in part by political sensitivities as much as factual uncertainty. In this political context, striving for a perfect answer may be practically impossible. You may need to confront the temporary reality that the "A" answer you believe in must sometimes be subordinated to the "B" answer you can make happen.

Probing for the relative importance and stress on different fault lines can be done in a very "consultative," indirect manner. For example, you might ask questions like,

- "So, how's business?" (I've found that how a person answers this is very telling. "Well, we're ten percent behind our sales goal" is a very different answer from "Well, my new CRM system is three months late," or "Our market share is down five percent," or "Really my biggest challenge is getting the team to come together.")

- "What are the most important, least-understood issues you're facing? Why are they the most important, and what do you think you need to know more about? How high is the burden of proof?" This is a good question to ask across the analyst/businessperson divide. It's not uncommon for the analytic agenda to be divorced from the issues that are top of mind for the operator. (More on how to keep those connected in Part III.) Also, it's often the case that analysts have higher bars for the precision of the analysis than the decision being supported requires.

- "What part of your experience or training called your attention to this issue? Is there a specific way of thinking about issues like this that you've applied, that points to this issue?" This question will help you gauge the degree of functional myopia that you'll need to overcome.

- "What are your current plans for doing something about this? What else needs to be done? What would you suggest gets de-emphasized to make room for that?"

Packaging for Balance: "The Analytic Brief"

While this gentle-probe approach, even as simplified as it is, may make sense to you while reading this, my experience has been that it's still not fit for consumption. To bring it to bear, you need to wrap it up in a single package. In our own work, we've developed such an artifact, which we call an "Analytic Brief." The executives interviewed for this book had their own various ways of metaphorically bundling their preferred approaches. We'll explore these further in Chapter 5,

"Practical Frameworks—For Getting on the Same Page," and in the conversations in Part IV "Conversations with Practitioners."

Visions for the Analytics Capability to Serve These Needs

So far, two things should start becoming clear. The first is that, in many ways, analysis is the easy part. Orchestrating analysis so that it isn't just acted upon, but welcomed as fundamental to driving decisions and actions, is often harder and more time consuming than actually doing the analysis itself. The second is that, in the service of this first objective, you may need to start with analysis that is simpler and more transparent, both because it's easier to orchestrate action around it, and because with less time and less rope (at least to start with), you can't take it to the most sophisticated levels. This has major implications for a lot of things, including the vendor solutions you select and the people you hire. But once again, a major theme of this book, echoed throughout all of the conversations that inform it, is that analysis has no intrinsic value—it's only useful if it's acted on. And you don't need to be absolutely right, you just need to be *better*. So one major attribute for any effective analytic capability is a practical orientation for progress and results.

As you move toward this practical orientation, a well-developed analytic capability is balanced across research, analysis, and testing. Managed in silos, practitioners of each of these techniques will stretch, at greater expense and with less certainty at potential insights. Statisticians will add variables of diminishing incremental explanatory power to models. Researchers will weight and re-weight survey responses to make up for sample shortcomings. Testing teams will stretch to multivariate scenarios that may be technically feasible but practically hard to coordinate and communicate. But managed together (or at least carefully coordinated), it's much easier to squeeze what's practical from each and switch to the next when the air starts getting too thin. Belinda Lang, former CMO of Aetna Insurance's consumer group, relied on all three of these levers in launching and growing various new business options in her twenty years at American Express, and she cites the balance among them as a key driver of the success those options had.

Some discussion questions:

- Which is your dominant analytic perspective?
- Which analytic perspective pre-dominates for your boss(es), peers, and team members?
- How does homogeneity or diversity help or hinder you? What have you caught or missed as a consequence?
- What do you have planned to further leverage or overcome this diversity or homogeneity?
- What organizational fault lines are most pronounced in your situation?
- Is your communication of analytic findings tuned for the fault line you're dealing with?

2

Access to Data—Too Often Taken for Granted

Getting to Data: Historical Models and Patterns

Here is a history of the Business-IT relationship in the realms of marketing and sales that more or less describes the average experience. Most firms will fall into a classic bell-curve distribution around this mean of the truth. Try to place yourself and your organization in this range to assess how much work is ahead of you to get to the data access you need.

The Paleo-Analytic Era

For most of the twentieth century, sales and marketing executives used relatively less accountable channels (including TV, print, radio, and events) to stimulate awareness, help somewhat more accountable channels (including direct mail and outbound phone) to generate leads, and then (directly or indirectly) drive sales. Because the less accountable channels used for "brand-building" didn't generate much data (aside from focus groups and ratings services), the executives managing them didn't need to be as numbers-oriented. Also, because of the lack of data on the impact of spending in these channels, there was more emphasis on buying these media as cheaply as possible. This meant volume purchases, through, for example, the spring "upfronts" that television networks use to sell ad time on their featured properties in the following fall. With media commitments locked up in advance, there were fewer degrees of freedom for tuning marketing efforts through these channels. And, with fewer adjustments, there were fewer opportunities to observe causes and effects and learn from them—which further reinforced limits to the development of data-oriented management. So the cycle went, for a long time.

On the direct marketing side, things were only a little better. Yes, we could record the productivity of calls and mail, and even, to a certain degree, the effectiveness of print ads and "Direct Response Television," with dedicated phone numbers ("Operators are standing by!"). But since information technology was relatively expensive, we tended to organize and support these efforts in silos to optimize efficiency. And with numbers viewed as unsexy among marketers, we isolated the people who tended businesses based on them, and the machines that churned those numbers out, often in suburban office parks where land or rent was cheaper and well away from the urban offices where debates about "the brand" took place.

Meanwhile, in many places IT organizations grew up in the finance function. So, even as IT staff managed an enabling capability, it also meant they frequently approached this capability from a perspective of "making the numbers tie" and from an inclination toward control, security, and efficiency—not necessarily openness and availability. Also, unlike sales and marketing, where "making the numbers" is a regular, perpetual source of pressure, IT as part of finance did not (ironically) face the same existential consideration; rather, it just had to live within its budget. Finally, IT was an arcane thing outsiders didn't understand, and its managers could seek refuge in that when inquisitors got too close. A senior media executive once ruefully expressed frustration to me about how, when he would probe software engineers in the IT department to try to understand why something wasn't working, was late, or over budget, "They would 'black box' me"—meaning they would answer questions using sufficient technical jargon as to make any insight and help from the business side impossible. This allowed the process of providing information to be dominated by an engineering mentality biased for emphasizing solid infrastructure, data quality, and governance foundations, versus repeated application and results. For transaction systems, this is good. For analytic applications, and for customer-facing sales and marketing interfaces that must constantly re-invent themselves to move customers toward those transactions, it's not.

The Meso-Analytic Era

By the late 1980s, more forward-thinking executives started to look across individual call and mail campaigns to track return on investment at the customer relationship level. This spawned consulting "thought leadership" and products that together comprised the CRM boom of the early 1990s. The core enabling capability at the heart of the trend was the Data Warehouse, linking customer information with sales results where possible. However, software licenses for Data Warehouse tools were expensive. Features bought crept beyond features needed. Integration challenges (for example, reconciling geographic territory definitions, such as "city" versus "Metropolitan Statistical Area") drove complex, lengthy, and therefore also expensive implementations. These attributes, along with increasingly shorter patience for results in the Age of the Leveraged Buyout, meant that a lot of Data Warehouse implementation efforts collapsed under their own weight. (Bain & Company partners Darrell Rigby and Dianne Ledingham described this dynamic very well in a 2004 *Harvard Business Review* article.[1]) These negative experiences had

---

[1] Darrell K. Rigby and Dianne Ledingham, "CRM Done Right," *Harvard Business Review*, November 2004, accessed at http://hbr.org/2004/11/crm-done-right/ar/1.

the effect of driving "business" and IT executives back to their own respective corners. Once again, without the tools to drive business results, and without the opportunities to learn how to use and apply them, business executives mostly didn't develop data skills. And IT executives, often without close relationships with business executives to connect them to specific users and use cases, tended to build highly generalized infrastructures, abstracted to anticipate a much broader range of requests than they would likely see, and generally taking too long to address specific opportunities when they presented themselves.

The Ceno-Analytic Era

By the mid to late 1990s, businesses were discovering the Internet. Three relevant patterns emerged. First was the rise of the "pure play" online firm. A whole new generation of sales and marketing executives grew up knowing nothing other than a data-rich, and therefore data-driven, environment. Second was the rise of "bolted-on" digital business units at traditional firms. These online adjuncts were often organizationally separated and physically isolated from the traditional elements of the business, and so they were able to cultivate cultures more removed from traditional "anti-data" biases. As these divisions grew at several times the rates of their traditional counterparts, they too created more (and more accelerated) career opportunities, both for younger, internally grown executives as well as recruits from the pure plays. Third, direct marketing became digital—primarily through the email channel.

Many of the primary data sources across all these groups were also, crucially, *not* provisioned by IT, though IT of course did play a selection and implementation role (for example, by page tagging). Rather, they came from web analytics and marketing automation providers who, in many if not most cases, provided their products as hosted, SAAS (Software-as-a-Service) solutions provisioned through browsers (think Google Analytics or Adobe *SiteCatalyst*, for example, on the analytic front; think vendors like Marketo, or even social media partners such as LinkedIn and Facebook, on the marketing execution front). SAAS provisioning made it possible to move faster and less expensively, since these vendors were already well ahead on the learning and scale curves for implementing the technology "stack" underlying their tools.

Modern Times

Finally, time and a now-critical mass of business through digital channels have begun to do their jobs. In many industries, these channels now predominate target segments' "experiences" across the pipeline. And, a new generation of senior leadership has grown up building and running these digital channels. Together, these two factors have moved data closer to the fore of marketing and analytics decision-making.

There's still room to go, however. Remember Talbots' Rob Schmults' earlier example: "If you go to a manager of a physical store," he says, "and you ask her, 'How's business?' she's unlikely to answer, 'Well, our project to deploy talking price tags is on schedule!'" What he means is that in many cases, if you ask this question of a manager of a digital channel, you're as likely to get an answer that has to do with the *capability* as you are an answer about the *result*. He attributes this to the fact that many of the senior *business* people now leading digital channels and businesses started out as managers of construction projects, on virgin virtual land.

Why does the "capability-builder" bias that Rob described matter? Building a marketing and sales capability in general, and improving data access in particular, is, in a reality we often miss, ignore, or deny, an organic process involving real people—not a mechanical one, as the executives who manage it are most likely to see it. The experiences I described above roll up into values—beliefs about how the world works (and doesn't)—which collectively form cultures. Working in an "If-we-build-it-they-will-come" culture is very different from one governed by objective, quantitatively expressed feedback loops. One of the features of the "Age of Analytics" is the ascendancy of these loops—the notion that decisions about what to build for a business or show to a prospective customer need to be informed by clear accountability to performance and cost. With feedback available as frequently as daily and even (through vendors like Chartbeat) in real time, even "build-oriented" executives are drawn to data like moths to the flame. And this availability then tends to set the bar for what the business expects IT to provide elsewhere.

Moving Forward

There are two ways to change cultures. One is to swap in people with the values you want. As David Norton says of his former boss, Gary Loveman, "When your CEO has a Ph.D. from MIT, it kind of sets the tone for the direction of the firm and helps the analysts there feel valued." The other is to change the experiences of the people you have, to re-shape their values. At La-Z-Boy, the CIO reports to Doug Collier, the CMO (an admittedly highly unusual structure that has much to do with Doug's abilities and his relationship with the CEO). This provides IT with a fully accountable seat at the marketing function's table.

Assuming you are predominantly down the second path of "dancing with them that brung you," what all this means—and this is a core point of this book—is that the typical "platform-first" way IT thinks about supporting analytics for marketing and sales (at least, if not other functions of the business as well) needs to be turned upside down. The first, bottom layer of any analytic "stack" for marketing and sales needs to be a collection of specific challenges and opportunities to pursue, and questions and tests related to them, ideally generated through the frameworks we suggest in Part II, "Practical

Analytics: Proven Techniques and Heuristics." The next layer up is a very general description of the data and data relationships necessary to answer these questions and support these tests, and, crucially, a plan for when you'll need this information and how much you can afford to spend on it, given the potential value of the different things you're pursuing. *Only then* should you start talking data models and logical system architectures. Figure 2.1 describes this graphically.

The Inverted Analytic Stack

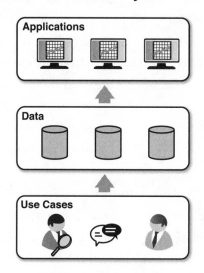

Figure 2.1   The Inverted Analytic Stack

Lenovo's "Analytic Maturity Model"

Lenovo's Mohammed Chaara suggests proceeding through an "analytic maturity model" that has these very properties. He says, "I start by working with the data that's already available. I actually avoid contact with IT at this stage." He does so because he observes that IT is typically resource-constrained and it makes more sense to see if there's a good case for investing in bigger infrastructure and better data to support an opportunity. Mo believes that "Any good analyst can extract value from dirty, incomplete data, at least enough to get a sense for whether there's value worth pursuing further." If there's a reason to continue, Mo's second analytic maturity stage is about further understanding the issues that come with the relevant data. These might include, for example, needs to reconcile master data hierarchies, or perhaps privacy constraints that will need to be imposed and administered (and perhaps audited) regularly. With these management requirements come governance needs as well. Emerging from this stage with clear requirements then allows Mo to proceed to a third stage, where IT can be productively engaged and focused on how to deliver against these requirements. Mo observes that the typical approach is exactly the opposite. Conversations start with, as he puts it, "foundation-planning": Often led by IT, the firm first inventories the data it has, and then determines how this data should be defined, physically maintained, and governed. Only once the foundation has been established is the storefront opened. Mo observes that, however, "The problem is that nine months later, you have nothing to show for it, in terms of any business insight or result."

Sharp-eyed readers will observe that in this case, Mo's analytic team is sufficiently sophisticated about data management and governance issues to be able to play a hybrid business/IT role, effectively playing the part of a team of business analysts that might typically be the tip of the spear for an IT organization. However, the difference here is that by organizing itself as a "Center of Excellence" growing out of the "business" side of the organization, the "tribal DNA" of the group orients itself first toward solving specific problems and filtering for the ones that have sufficient value to be worth supporting more robustly. Business analysts coming out of IT, in my own experience and that of others who addressed this issue for this book, rarely start there. They tend to "take orders" to explore the data implications for a business opportunity without clear vetting of that opportunity. This is true even if there is a "business case" form involved in submitting the order; often the authors of those business cases are either not well analytically supported or they are not impartial.

Building the Data Warehouse

To summarize, the bottom layer/first stage described previously is typically called "requirements gathering." However, the ways functional and technical requirements have traditionally been expressed have focused more on features, specifications, and (occasionally) performance, not on capturing and tightly linking the business needs—users and use cases—these are meant to support. Buried in the second edition of what is widely accepted as the bible on the subject, Ralph Kimball's *The Data Warehouse Toolkit*, in the middle of Chapter 16, is a section titled "Common Data Warehousing Mistakes to Avoid."[2] Woven throughout the ten mistakes listed there is a common theme: De-coupling data warehouse development from cheek-by-jowl participation in solving real business problems is a recipe for disaster.

The stakes for getting this wrong are higher than ever. The data sets are bigger, their sources and quality are more varied, the holy wars among advocates of different technologies for wrangling them are nastier, and so governance has gone from something that could move on its own schedule to something that needs to work, practically, and now. So how do you build a data warehouse today, in a way that simultaneously addresses, on the one hand, exploding volume/variety/velocity, and on the other, the fluidity with which business opportunities that depend on data-driven insights appear and vanish?

Today, answers to this question might start with, "Well, first you implement Hadoop to store and summarize your data, and then you use Hive to query it..." We'll get to what's relevant about the technology in a moment. But the first order of business is to think carefully about the data you actually need. The following story illustrates the dramatic difference this can make.

---

[2] Kimball, Ralph, and Ross, Margy, *The Data Warehouse Toolkit*, Wiley: 2002, p. 366

The BENS "BRN" Story

In 2004, Ern Blackwelder, a friend and former colleague, was working at a Washington, DC-based non-profit called Business Executives for National Security (BENS). BENS was asked by the Democratic National Committee to help set up a "Business Response Network" (BRN) to support the security and disaster recovery needs of the 2004 Democratic National Convention in Boston.[3] The BRN collected commitments from large local businesses to provide relevant people and assets to the Massachusetts Emergency Management Agency (MEMA) in case of a large-scale disaster following, say, a terrorist attack (for example: the aftermath of blowing up the weekly liquid natural gas (LNG) tanker shipment that comes into Boston Harbor). Rather than having the Department of Homeland Security purchase, transport, and stage emergency response assets such as trucks, generators, bulldozers, office space, and communications equipment, the idea was to pre-enlist local businesses with these assets, pre-negotiate liability limitations, and pre-register relevant assets so they could be brought to bear if needed.

The idea presented two major challenges. The first was creating a unified, up-to-date database to register and track thousands of committed assets. Different firms had "asset management systems" of different maturities (some were highly digital and tracked the location of, say, a truck with GPS-enabled transponders; others used paper based systems akin to library cards). The second was that BENS had six weeks, and a five-figure budget, to get the job done.

There's a saying: "You can have good, quick, and cheap. Pick two." However, the saying assumes scope is given. The BENS team re-thought the problem. What Ern and his colleagues realized was that they could parse what it meant to *track* commitments. So, they

---

[3] Peter J. Howe, "State Firms Form Groups For Disaster Response," *Boston Globe*, July 24, 2004, accessed at http://pqasb.pqarchiver.com/boston/doc/404922349.html.

created three categories of assets. For the first, merely having contact information for the people responsible (say, a primary and one or two backups) for them would be sufficient. BENS didn't—or practically, couldn't—track the quantity and location of these assets. However, a text, email, or phone call to a responsible person could summon them readily, so that didn't matter. For the second category, BENS added a "main location," with directions and access instructions, to go along with the contact information for responsible parties in case direct and immediate access was necessary. And for the third group, in the case of unique, specialized equipment (certain HAZMAT equipment, for example), BENS registered not just the general descriptions of the available assets, but checked and updated their specific locations at regular intervals.

This approach had several advantages. First, and most important, it vastly reduced the amount of work needed by the companies participating in the BRN to provide the necessary information initially and to keep it fresh. Second, it reduced the amount of work needed by the BENS team to take in and administer this information. And third, it reduced the cost and complexity of the technology footprint needed to support the effort, to the point where the whole thing could be implemented in a matter of days and for a few hundred dollars through one of the early, cloud-based database services of the day, by technically competent but not necessarily expert businesspeople on the team. The punch line: The BENS team was able to recruit and register commitments worth $300 million from over two dozen firms in less than three weeks, well within its budget—a tiny fraction of what it would otherwise have cost to provide this degree of support if they hadn't re-scoped the requirements of the service.

What can we take away from this? The database created by the BENS team had very specific use cases informing it. The design of the database considered very carefully the tradeoffs between the marginal value of different types of information about assets and the costs, direct and indirect, of providing and maintaining that information.

And finally, the database was created by people whose understanding of the challenges at hand was deep enough to allow them to "wrangle" the necessary technical requirements to a simplified, manageable scope—so much so that it entered the realm of something they could, with a little energy and willingness to Read The Manual, build the necessary solution themselves.

A common objection by experienced developers of data warehouses would be that hacks like this don't scale across a broader range of needs, and that by not anticipating that breadth and engineering for it, it would ultimately be much more expensive to re-build the necessary solution. Today, with tools like Hadoop and cheap cloud-based infrastructure to run it on, one might well add, "Just store first and ask questions later." This may well have merit. However, there is no scenario under which gathering requirements and prototyping them under the guidance of Einstein's "Everything should be as simple as possible, but no simpler" dictum, within this little time and cost, and for so much immediate benefit, short-changes the future. Rather, it makes the future more likely, by giving it a foundational story, a business case, and a real-world sense of what's actually needed for the task at hand.

Implications for Big Data Investments

So now let's come back to Big Data. You may (and probably do) need a Big Data wrangling capability. Just don't buy it on spec. "Govern" it with specific use cases. Fund and evolve it on shoestring budgets and time cycles. Evaluate it based on the demonstrated value of tests associated with the use cases you develop.

This is particularly important because a leading strain of thinking in the Big Data end of the marketing and analytics sales pool is to pursue what some call an "emergent" strategy. That is, assemble a big data set, then let the machines explore all the possibilities and tell you what relationships are significant. What the executives interviewed for this book have learned is that applying the "emergent" approach needs to be scoped and governed carefully by broader hypotheses. For example, one said (off the record in order not to leak a competitive advantage), "We developed a hypothesis that geography matters to marketing mix allocation because of A, B, and C. We started by validating that generally, through sampling. Then we asked, 'Which aspects of geographies matter most?' and pursued a machine learning approach for that, to generate models that can help us decide which geographies matter more for which decisions under different conditions." A popular example of this balance, documented by Charles Duhigg in his book *The Power of Habit* and first reported in *The New York Times*,[4] is Target's marketing to expectant mothers. Framed by the question, "What do recent purchases by expectant mothers tell us they might like next?" statisticians there were able to identify relevant collections of products whose purchases communicated varying propensities to purchase other products, and target offers accordingly.

One reason this careful attention to governance is necessary is because in the world of Big Data, pre-processing raw data to add meaning necessary for interpretation is typically a big part of the work to be done, and re-doing this pre-processing can sometimes be time-consuming. (The good news of course is that it's now more practically feasible in technical and financial terms, compared with using conventional relational database management system (RDBMS)-based approaches.) Here's an example: Let's say you want to track trends in sentiment about your firm across a variety of social media, for later correlation with purchase trends. Through a variety of means (scraping, RSS, APIs, and so on), you slurp in a large stream of raw text. You use Hadoop to store it, and you write Hadoop MapReduce scripts to analyze and classify bits of raw text as "positive" or "negative," along

---

[4] Charles Duhigg, "How Companies Learn Your Secrets," *The New York Times*, February 16, 2012, accessed at http://www.nytimes.com/2012/02/19/magazine/shopping-habits.html.

with placing them in time and adding other metadata like source, and context. Then you organize the processed version of this data, using, say, a NoSQL database—such as Apache HBase, or a commercially-supported alternative such as MapR's M7, for example if you're using the sentiment trend conclusions to drive automated real-time recommendations. This ends up looking like: "On June 25, person X on site Y said a 'positive' thing about us while discussing topic Z." Then the data can be further queried: "What's the trend in the number of 'positive' things said about us in sites like Y in the context of topics like Z during the summer?" One challenge here is that programmers need to learn new languages, like Pig, to run these queries. Another challenge is that if you want to apply a more nuanced range of meaning for sentiment—say, move from simply "positive" or "negative" to introduce "neutral", for example—you need to redo the pre-processing of your raw data. This is getting easier as different Big Data vendors integrate their technology stacks—abstract away multiple programming layers and make everything run more efficiently—but it's why it still pays to think a bit up front.

(Aside: What's Big Data?)

Some common questions executives ask include, "What exactly is Big Data? Are there official volume and other thresholds for it? Does the data itself have any particular properties?" At this point, while many can point to drivers, such as volume, velocity of incoming data, and variety of sources it comes from, there are no clear borders.

Rather, Big Data is defined more by the experience of working with it. For example, if a query on a data sample takes hours to run on an enterprise-class implementation of a relational database management system (RDBMS), and further scaling that solution to larger sample or the full universe of relevant data would cost hundreds of thousands of dollars, then you may have a Big Data challenge that would benefit from newer, more relevant tools that scale much more cheaply.

A variant of this answer suggests the following triage:

- If you can load a relevant data set into your PC's memory and run your analysis there using tools like Microsoft Excel or Access, with response times for your queries staying within a minute or so, you're firmly in Small Data land. Pushed for a rule of thumb, experts would say data set sizes here would stay within a million records.

- If your analysis involves running queries against a single instance of a relational database consisting mostly of well-structured data, running on a single conventional server, or even a small cluster administered by a small team, and your response time for a typical query is still "reasonable" (let's say well inside an hour), you're still well within the boundaries of "conventional" data processing. Sizes of data sets managed this way can run to tens or even hundreds of millions of records—assuming they consist of well-structured data.

- Once your queries begin to take longer than this to run, you begin to lose analytic flexibility. Simply put, you can't iterate as easily. At this point you are (at least in terms of the challenge) in the world of Big Data. To deal with it you have three choices:

    1. Try to scale your conventional relational database infrastructure to keep up. However, this quickly becomes impractical in terms of cost, even if you can manage the complex IT administration logistics.

    2. Migrate to sophisticated "appliances" from vendors such as Netezza (now owned by IBM) that integrate highly specialized combinations of hardware and software to keep performance within acceptable bounds.

    3. Take advantage of a new generation of open-source tools (with varying degrees of commercial support), collectively referred to as "NoSQL." These are spun out from technologies developed at Google, Yahoo!, Amazon, and

Facebook; the common denominator across these technologies is their ability to harness massively parallel computing resources underneath them. Essentially, to scale their performance to larger and larger data sets, you simply keep adding processors for them to run on. Also, these processors can be provisioned as virtual machines running on cloud infrastructures for even greater convenience.

Supporting Ad Hoc Approaches to Defining Data Requirements

My friend Tip Clifton is CEO of Eastport Analytics, a boutique firm in Arlington, Virginia, across the river from DC's Georgetown. He and his colleagues have developed some very sophisticated applications for helping the government track and catch terrorists and tax cheats. But arguably more interesting is the approach they take to developing these applications.

Tip describes two main insights that have driven their work. The first was inspired by his brother-in-law, an ophthalmologist: "The process for determining your prescription is iterative," Tip says. "They keep flipping lenses in front of your eyes, and eventually you settle on strengths that allow you to see most clearly. Our approach to requirements is similar. In general, people are better at reacting than acting. So, we don't ask our users to tell us what they want from the outset. Rather, we grab some data, and we iterate ways of presenting this information that most effectively answer their questions."

The second insight relates to how they stage the data to do this. "Many of the modern visualization tools—Tableau and Spotfire are a couple of examples—allow you to create dashboards or workbooks that can simultaneously connect to multiple, independent data sources that can range from huge relational databases and web services to Microsoft Access databases and Excel worksheets. So, we don't worry initially about creating a single *physical* data store—a data warehouse—for the 'optometry exam.' Rather, we construct a *logical* abstraction of a warehouse—we call it an Intelligence Repository. Basically it's a neatly organized directory that points to the available data. We dump whatever hodgepodge our client's got into that and prototype our solutions from that foundation. Once our users have a better idea of what they actually want, we can work on performance and data governance. But for our users, it's sort of like plugging into an electrical outlet. When the bulb goes on, they don't know, and mostly don't care, whether the juice is coming from a portable generator or a nuclear power station. It's just illuminating their work." Consider how Tip's firm's approach generally, and the Intelligence Repository in particular, is complementary to the process Mo Chaara follows at Lenovo.

These experiences suggest that traditional "monolithic" IT approaches to managing data can be usefully unpacked into four levels: communication, coordination, collaboration, and control. At the simplest level, "communication," governance can be as basic as registering the existence relevant data sets in a commonly accessible place; just as firms publish organization charts and floor maps, imagine if they also published basic directories of what's collected and who has it. Next up, "coordination" implies that at minimum, two different groups don't bump into each other unproductively as they separately work with a shared data set. For example, this could mean scheduling access times or making each other aware of conversations with relevant vendors that each might benefit from separately. Further on, "collaboration" can mean working together to make a bundled purchase of necessary data at a lower price, or even on agreeing on some common ways to define and organize data for mutual benefit. Finally, "control" means someone gets the final call on the definition and disposition of data. As shown in Figure 2.2, this four-level model reconciles business-driven opportunity exploration with IT-driven attention to foundation by defining expectations each might have of the other at different analytic maturity stages. Crossed with Mo Chaara's analytic maturity stages, it can serve both diagnostic and pre-scriptive purposes.

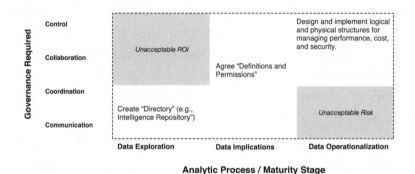

Figure 2.2   Analytic Process Governance Diagnosis and Prescription

Managing External Sources

These days much of the data you might like to include in your analysis is not on your servers but on some media partner's (your agency's, a social network, or a publisher if you're working directly with one), a Software-as-a-Service provider's (for example, Salesforce, Marketo, and so on), or is accessed from public sources (for example, economic series from the St. Louis Federal Reserve Bank[5]). Some of these organizations—typically agencies—may already be providing you with highly summarized reports in inflexible formats. If you ask for regular access to more granular data, they may try to charge you for that. In that scenario, you're often better off offering to trade the

---

[5] "FRED API," St. Louis Fed Web Services, http://api.stlouisfed.org/docs/fred/.

(typically less useful) reports currently provided for the raw data, and then using more powerful data wrangling and visualization tools to allow you to re-build your old reports and extend them with additional dimensionality (that is, make them more "drillable" than before).

As more branding dollars go to digital channels via trends such as "content marketing,"[6] a good example of data you're likely to want more often would be display ad impression and click data from ad servers. A typical Excel-based report you would get from an agency might simply summarize activity (impressions and clicks) in given periods, along with the budgets expended in those periods. But, for the purposes of attribution or other kinds of analysis, you might be interested in finer-grained dates and times, as well as more detail about the publisher, ad unit, creative, and other dimensions. Of course you'll have to honor any privacy-related restrictions.

So far we've assumed you want to bring data from these external sources in-house. However, depending on the "center of gravity" sales and marketing channels for your business, it might be best to add your data to the analytical repository your partner provides, as long as you make sure you have the access to it you want. For example, in a business that uses primarily a direct sales model, and which uses a hosted "Sales Force Automation" solution like Salesforce.com, it might be most useful to simply add certain data (service data, for example) there if it's not already in.

The common denominator in these scenarios is explicit, detailed discussion up front and on an ongoing basis with any vendor about access to (formats, service levels) and costs of data generated through the use of the vendor's tools and services. At the same time, it's important to come to some agreement with IT about a vision and roadmap for what must come in-house.

---

[6] "Content Marketing," *Wikipedia*, http://en.wikipedia.org/wiki/Content_marketing.

Some questions for discussion:

- You want to profile "near-converters" on your web site, so you can tune a re-targeting campaign for them that includes demographically appropriate messaging and product recommendations based on collaborative filtering. That's three data sources: customer file, sales file, web analytics. What's your starting point for this analysis? Choose from one of the following answers:

    1. We have to source and integrate the data from the underlying transaction systems.

    2. We have a data warehouse that combines the first and second sources, along with a highly-summarized version of the third that unfortunately tells us whether someone's registered on our site, not whether they fall into a "near converter" cohort.

    3. We have a highly advanced Big Data platform, and with about a day's work we can generate a re-targeting list for use by our marketing teams.

    4. Targeting near-converters with certain demographic characteristics and offering them discounts on related products based on surfing patterns and demographic profiles is an algorithm our machine-learning infrastructure has deemed promising through automated testing.

- Where along this spectrum do you feel your greatest leverage lies, based on similar specific use cases you think might have value and that you could feasibly implement with the team and resources you have today?

- Where do you feel you need to be in 12 months, and what market or competitive examples do you see that shape your thinking?

3

Operational Flexibility—Don't Analyze What You Can't Act On

Analytic insights have no value if they can't be put to work. Melanie Murphy, Director of Analytics for the home goods retailer Bed Bath & Beyond, says, "If you can't act on the model, you probably shouldn't build it." This chapter describes and explores dimensions of marketing and sales processes and infrastructure so managers and executives on both sides of the analysis/operations divide can properly time their investments in their respective capabilities to make sure they aren't idle while they wait on each other.

Marketing operations limitations come in several different shapes. You may discover certain differences in customer demographics or behavior that predict purchase or some other target action. But you may lack a marketing automation platform that can react quickly enough, with sufficiently fine-grained pricing or messaging, to take advantage of these differences during relevant time windows. Or, the systems you do have may not be functioning as they should because of imperfect maintenance (a failure to whitelist your mail server, for example).

Three scenarios emerge from the conversations for this book.

1. You don't have the marketing and sales automation machinery to execute tests or solutions for the insights you've developed.

2. You have the machinery, but either it's not fully implemented or the processes that support it (for example, getting creative

content developed for testing a landing page variant) are still done "the old way."

3. You have the machinery, but there's a line to stand in for resources, and you have to take a number.

We'll look at each of these in turn to describe challenges you might run into and how to deal with them.

As with the need to find common analytic frameworks to drive strategic alignment discussed in Chapter 1, "Strategic Alignment," any successful effort to match operational flexibility to analytic capability has to start with a common understanding of the operations that the analysis might impact. So, what is marketing and sales automation? What capabilities does it include? What should you get first, next, later? Lots of vendors, including big ones such as IBM, Oracle, and TeraData, as well as hundreds more, are now investing in answering these questions, especially as they try to reach beyond IT to sell directly to the Chief Marketing Officer (CMO). These vendors provide myriad marketing materials to describe both the landscape and their products, which variously are described as "campaign management systems" or even more gloriously as "marketing automation solutions." The proliferation of solutions is so mind-blowing that analyst firms build whole practices making sense of the category. For example, Terence Kawaja's very popular "LUMAscape" charts illustrate the relevant domains memorably and comprehensively.[1]

A "Common Requirements Framework"

Yet even with this guidance, organizations struggle to get relevant stakeholders on the same page about what's needed and how to proceed. My own experience has been that this is because they're

---

[1] "Lumascapes," Luma Partners, http://www.lumapartners.com/resource-center/lumascapes-2/.

missing a simple "Common Requirements Framework" that everyone can share as a point of departure for the conversation. Here's one I've found useful.

Basically, marketing is about *targeting* the right customers and getting them the right *content* (product information, pricing, and all the before-during-and-after trimmings) through the right *channels* at the right *time*. So, for example, a *marketing automation* solution, well, automates this. More specifically, since there are lots of homegrown hacks and point solutions for different pieces of this, what's really getting automated is the manual conversion and shuffling of files from one system to the next, or in other words, the integration of it all. Some of these solutions also let you run analyses and tests out of the same platform (or partnered components).

Each of these functions has increasing levels of sophistication; I've characterized them into "basic," "threshold," and "advanced." For simple road mapping and prioritization purposes, you might also call these "now," "next," and "later."

Targeting

The simplest form of targeting uses a single data source—past experience at the cash register—to decide whom to go back to, on the idea that you build a business inside out from your best, most loyal customers. Cataloguers have a fancy term for this: "RFM," which stands for "Recency, Frequency, and Monetary Value." RFM grades customers, typically into deciles, according to, well, how recently, how frequently, and how much they've bought from you. Folks who score high get solicited more intensively (for example, more catalog drops). By looking back at a customer's past RFM-defined marginal value to you (the gross margin you earned from stuff you sold her), you can make a decision about how much to spend marketing to her.

One step up, you add demographic and behavioral information about customers and prospects to refine and expand your lists of folks to target. Demographically, for example, you might say, "Hey, my best customers all seem to come from Greenwich, CT. Maybe I should target other folks who live there." You might add a few other dimensions to that, such as age and gender. Or you might buy synthetic, "psychographic" definitions from data vendors who roll a variety of demographic markers into inferred attitudes. Behaviorally, you might say, "Let's *retarget* folks who walk into our store or who put stuff into our online shopping cart but don't check out." These are conceptually straightforward things to do, but they are logistically harder because now you have to integrate external and internal data sources, comply with privacy policies, and so on.

In the third level, you begin to formalize the models implicit in these prior two steps and build lists of folks to target based on their predicted propensity to buy (lots) from you. For example, you might say, "Folks who bought this much of this product this frequently, this recently, who live in Greenwich, and who visited our web site last week, have this probability of buying this much from me, so therefore I can afford to target them with a marketing program that costs X dollars per person." That's "predictive modeling."

Some folks evaluate the sophistication of a targeting capability by how fine-grained the target segments get, or by how close to 1-1 personalization you can get. In my experience, there are often diminishing returns to this, often because the firm can't always practically execute differentiated experiences, even if the marginal value of a personalized experience warrants it. This isn't universally the case of course: Promotional offers and similar experience variables (for example, credit limits) are easier to vary than, say, a hotel lobby.

Content

Again, a simple progression exists here, for me defined by the complexity of the content you can provide ("plain," "rich," "interactive," and so on) and by the flexibility and precision ("none," "pre-defined options," "custom options," and so on) with which you can target the content through any given channel or combination of channels. Wayfair's Ben Clark offered a particularly rich illustration of the cutting edge of this dimension in our conversation for this book (see Chapter 14, "Conversations with Practitioners").

Another content dimension to consider is the complexity of the organizations and processes necessary to produce this content. For example, in highly regulated environments like health care or financial services, you may need multiple approvals before you can publish something. And the more folks involved, the more sophisticated and valuable the coordination tools, ranging from central repositories for templates, version control systems, alerts, and even joint editing. Beware, though, of simply paving cow paths—be sure you need all that content variety and process complexity before enabling it technologically, or it will simply expand to fit what the technology permits (the same way computer operating systems bloat as processors get more powerful).

Channels

The big dimension here is the number of channels you can string together for an integrated experience. For example, in a simple case you have one channel, say email, to work with. In a more sophisticated system, you can say, "When people who look like this come to our website, retarget them with ads in the display ad network we use." (Google recently integrated Google Analytics with Google Display Network to do just this,[2] an ingenious move that further illustrates why they lead the pack in the display ad world.) Pushing it even further, you could also say, "In addition to retargeting website visitors

---

[2] "Features," Google Analytics, http://www.google.com/analytics/features/remarketing.html.

who do X out in our display network, let's also send them an email/ postcard combination with connections to a landing page or phone center."

Analysis and Testing

In addition to *execution* of campaigns and programs, a marketing solution might also support *evaluation and exploration* of what campaigns and programs, or components thereof, might work best. This happens in a couple of ways. You can examine past behavior of customers and prospects to look for trends and build models that explain how changes and saliencies along one or more dimensions might have been associated with buying. Also, you can define and execute A/B and multivariate tests (with control groups) for targeting, content, and channel choices.

Again, the question here is not just about how much data flexibility and algorithmic power you have to work with within the system, but how many integration hoops you have to go through to move from exploration to execution. Obviously you won't want to run exploration and execution off the same physical data store, or even the same logical model, but it shouldn't take a major IT initiative to flip the right operational switches when you have an insight you'd like to try, or a successful experiment you'd like to scale to cover more of your customers.

Concretely, the requirement you're evaluating here is best summarized by a couple of questions. First, "Show me how I can track and evaluate differential responses in the marketing campaigns and programs I execute through your proposed solution," and then, "Show me how I can define and test targeting, content, and channel variants of the base campaigns or programs, and then work the winners into a dominant share of our mix."

A Summary Picture

See Figure 3.1 for a simple table that tries to bundle all this up. Notice that, in contrast with representations such as Terence Kawaja's LUMAscapes, it focuses more on function than features and capabilities instead of components. Also, in terms of the progression it describes, it is equally applicable to sales as to marketing.

	Basic/Now	Threshold/Next	Advanced/Later
Targeting	Simple / 1 data source used for targeting, outcomes-gased, e.g., "RFM"	Additional demographic and behavioral data	Formal predictive modeling used for targeting
Content	"Flat", e.g., text + graphics, minimal personalization	"Rich", e.g., video, pre-defined personalization	Interactive, e.g., apps, polls, surveys, calculators; custom, real-time personalization
Channels	1-2 channels, e.g., direct mail to phone, email to landing page	3+ channels, within a single function's control (e.g., Marketing)	3+ channels, integration across multiple organizational functions and partners
Analysis / Testing	Limited integration of analytics (basic, pre-defined reporting), manual testing	Integrated, flexible reporting, automated A/B testing	Well-integrated modeling, integrated multivariate testing

Figure 3.1   Common Requirements Framework for Marketing and Sales Automation

What's Right for You?

The important thing to remember is that these functions and capabilities are *means* not *ends*. To figure out what you need, you should reflect first on how any particular combination of capabilities would fit into your marketing organization's "vector and momentum." How is your marketing performance trending? How does it compare with competitors? In what parts (targets, content, and channels) is it better or worse? What have you deployed recently and learned through its operation? What kind of track record have you established in terms of successful deployment and leverage from your efforts?

If your answers are not strong or clear, then you might be better off signing onto a mostly-integrated, cloud-based (so you don't compound business value uncertainty with IT risk), good-enough-across-most-things solution for a few years until you sort out—affordably (read: rent, don't buy)—what works for you and what capability you need to go deep on. If, on the other hand, you're confident you have a good grip on where your opportunities are and you have momentum and confidence in your team, you might add best-of-breed capabilities at the margins of the more general "logical model" this proposed framework provides. What's generally risky is to start with an underperforming operation built on spaghetti and plan for a smooth multiyear transition to a fully integrated on-premise option—that just puts too many moving parts into play, with too high of an up-front, bet-on-the-come investment.

Again, remember that the point of a "Common Requirements Framework" isn't to serve as an exhaustive checklist for evaluating vendors. It's best used as a simple model you can carry around in your head and share with others, so that when you *do* dive deep into requirements, you don't lose the forest for the trees, in a category that's become quite a jungle.

Integrating Analytics into Operational Capability Planning

As we discussed in Chapter 1, we've observed three different analytic perspectives at work in marketing and sales. With marketing operations and planning for those operations sometimes organized separately from analytics groups, plans for what to build next can also often be divorced from groups that analyze and report how well existing capabilities are performing. As a consequence of this, the requirements for these systems to support ongoing analytics and testing can also be an afterthought. Even the tools themselves reinforce this balkanization. How else to explain why most modern content management systems still have not integrated testing as a native feature? It could be, for example, that the vendors behind these systems cannily play on the organizational silos. After all, it's likely more profitable to divide and conquer by selling the CMS to the operators and the A/B testing platform after the fact to a different group.

The charter of the modern analytics group is evolving to influence not just analytic capabilities but execution-oriented ones as well. Lenovo's Mo Chaara describes how for certain "chartered" analytic initiatives, such as determining indicators and causes for potentially "pervasive quality issues," his group's charge is to go all the way from exploring data for insights to standing up the platforms through which the opportunity will be realized. Generally this means being comprehensively involved at least through an operational pilot, in order to shake out all the bugs in practice. He describes this expansive role for the analyst as "the beginning of a new way of business management, where an analytics team leads the development of solutions that drive strategy," as opposed to simply reporting and analyzing the results after they happen. Paul Magill's newly centralized marketing intelligence function at Abbott provides another example of this modern role for the analytics group; there, Paul is counting on that team to inform the capabilities of Abbott's investments in digital channels, and in particular to make them as relevant for brand marketing as they have been for direct efforts.

Some discussion questions:

- How in sync (or not) are your analytic and execution capabilities?
- Which one is further ahead? How, and how far?
- What's your current plan for closing the gap?

- Is that plan an appropriate leap, or too short or too far?
- Along which dimension of execution—targeting, creative, channel, and so on—do you think your greatest opportunities lie?
- Are your current efforts aimed at this opportunity?
- If not, what can you do to adjust course?
- To what degree are you technology-constrained versus people-constrained?

4

People and Organization— Cultivate "Analytic Marketers"

The dominant tendency in marketing organizations is to draw charts first and then define and hire narrow roles into them. This is because the range of functions to be encompassed in a marketing organization is broad, and the knowledge required to execute each can be somewhat specialized. Inevitably, this leads to a situation where marketing analysts are uniquely defined and functionally segregated from other marketing roles. What follows is a too-common pattern: More numerate marketing analysts generate reports that less numerate marketers often don't use. In short, Venusians and Martians remain on their respective planets, without communicating effectively.

The advent of digital channels and the data they offer has made numbers somewhat less escapable. In "pure play" digital firms, numbers are oxygen for all marketers. Consider the case of the online home furnishings retailer Wayfair, where, in 2013, CEO Niraj Shah said that half his marketing staff knew how to use SQL to query the firm's data for the information they needed. In firms where digital channels have been developed on top of pre-existing channels, progress is somewhat slower.

In *Pragmalytics*, I suggested that the "org-first" approach to designing marketing organizations was precisely backward. I advocated for attracting strong, numerate generalists, and for providing training and constant application of numbers-driven marketing for both newcomers and existing team members. One way is to insist on having conversations across marketing and sales functions at the lowest possible plain-language common denominator. Both of these functions have, for many reasons, and not uniquely, evolved jargon-rich languages to which even experienced practitioners struggle to adapt when they move from shop to shop, since the same thing might go by several different situation-specific labels. For example, what, specifically, do we include when we say "SPIFF" (where does a short-term sales incentive stop, and become part of the broader comp plan?) or "DSP" (precisely what functions are we supporting through our digital advertising demand side platform)?

Recruiting

Today's conventional story tells us that, despite the U.S.'s lowest labor force participation rate in 35 years (as one proxy), there are hundreds of thousands of unfilled "quant" jobs in the country. Compensation trends bear this out.[1] The conventional solutions are to either increase your bid or to lower your expectations.

However, a more illuminated understanding of the analytic process would drive toward recruiting and cultivating a different set of people. First, it's important to recognize that only a small part of a marketing and sales challenge involves developing descriptive models and predictive algorithms. A lot of time is often consumed beforehand in gathering and staging data, examining trends and distributions visually, and packaging any relevant information and insights for communication and application afterward. Second, as we discussed in Chapter 3, "Operational Flexibility—Don't Analyze What You Can't Act On," a smart analytic strategy starts simply and doesn't expand

---

[1] "Statistical Analyst Salary," Indeed.com, http://www.indeed.com/salary/Statistical-Analyst.html.

any faster than a firm's ability to absorb and execute on insights it generates. Accordingly, your staffing efforts should recognize and follow this pattern, focusing more on smart, analytic generalists who can learn a range of directions and then leverage specialized skills at the edges of the work, via small internal cadres or external partners, rather than trying to stuff these resources in at the core and have analytic Ferraris running in first and second gear all the time and burning out their clutches.

Virtually all the conversations for this book bear this suggestion out. Belinda Lang, former CMO of Aetna's consumer business and a long-time executive at American Express, who at one point managed a team of fifty statisticians, valued "entrepreneurial" as much "analytical" in the people she recruited for her teams, who, coincidentally, included the future Harrah's CMO (and *CMO* Magazine 2010 CMO of the Year) David Norton. David himself noted how the ability to understand context and implications around analysis is a very important success factor there. He describes the head of his statistical modeling group as "a brilliant guy from the University of Nevada at Reno, who really was as much a strategic analytic marketer as he was a statistician. He really understood the marketing realities behind the numbers." Ben Clark at Wayfair notes significant levels of cross-disciplinary fluency: statisticians who can program, programmers who get models.

Nonetheless, reality intrudes. In a world where the renaissance generalist comes at a premium, if you can find one, Melanie Murphy focuses on finding well-qualified specialists—say a modeler and a database specialist—and teaming them closely and carefully. But even she screens for the ability to get your own data and communicate what your analysis means. The moral: Don't relax your recruiting approach or standards, even as you are creative about how your overall team is put together.

Skill Mix

Notwithstanding, while David Norton attracted many ex-consultants from Bain and McKinsey to Harrah's, he observes that the firm developed a strong preference for a profile that was "less Harvard" and "more Carnegie Mellon." This meant they de-emphasized subjective speculation about potential investments supported by "light" market research and put more stock in rigorous examination of behavioral data provided by their own customers' interactions with Harrah's at its properties. This in turn requires data wrangling skills—specifically, the ability to access, audit, adjust, and arrange data for subsequent analysis—that up the ante for the people you can recruit into an analytics group. At La-Z-Boy, with its headquarters in Monroe, Michigan, about 40 miles south of Detroit and a few blocks west of Lake Erie, CMO Doug Collier notes that it can be harder to find qualified recruits, and so he's had to get more creative to fill needed jobs. He's been looking at the firm's finance and engineering teams as potential sources for analysts who are especially curious and eager to expand their professional horizons. Another approach is to set the bar higher for marketers and provide training to help them clear it. For example, One way Wayfair CEO Niraj Shah achieved the high levels of database literacy described earlier was to put over half of the firm's marketing team through an introduction to SQL class[2] so they could crunch their own numbers.

Assuming you can wrangle the data, next up is the ability to analyze it. In Chapter 1, "Strategic Alignment—First You Need to Agree On What to Ask," we describe a basic analytic pathway any executive can apply. Beyond these skills lie techniques we rely on the pros to provide. However, as we look for and develop these, Scott McDonald's experience at Condé Nast suggests it's important to stay aware

---

[2] Wayfair has its own internally developed curriculum; you might start here, with the very accessible one provided by W3Schools: http://www.w3schools.com/sql/sql_intro.asp.

of potential biases that come with academically trained statisticians you might think to hire. As Scott puts it, "I came up as a statistically-trained sociologist, baptized in the Church Of The Random Sample and educated in The School Of The Normal Distribution." But, he observed in our conversations that the base case taught in academic statistics settings—random (unbiased) samples producing bell-curve distributions—is less common in the world of sales and marketing. The problem, Scott observes, is that many analysts today that grapple with big data sets start, rather blindly, with summary statistics about data sets that implicitly assume the academic base case, rather than the marketing and sales realities of biased samples and skewed distributions.

Scott pointed to Nate Silver's analysis of recent elections as a good example of the "arbitrage" these assumptions offer. By studying and handicapping the sampling biases of various polls, Silver was able to call each election right down to the very electoral vote count. In our conversation, he suggested how his analytic approach identifies and adjusts for these hidden biases. His ideas offer the basis for useful screening questions ("Tell me about the data you worked with—what assumptions did you make about it, and what adjustments did you have to make to it, in order to understand what had happened and make predictions from that?"), or a training curriculum ("Here are the characteristics of data sets we encounter in our corner of the sales and marketing domain...").

Marketing and sales analytics should of course be construed more broadly, extending to research and testing as well. There's a tendency, as we discuss in Part II, "Practical Analytics: Proven Techniques and Heuristics," to organize these capabilities in silos. If each group is then left to develop on its own, there's a risk that it might recruit past the point of diminishing returns in its silo. At any given point in time, the best marginal hire might be in another analytic discipline. For example, your next best move might not be a Ph.D. statistician, but rather a recent MBA with two or three years' experience designing and executing tests. In Part III, "Making Progress," we describe an approach to managing a portfolio of analytic initiatives that can help you decide who your next hire should be.

Here's a short checklist of skills, traits, and experiences to look for across your team, if not in an individual analyst:

- **Database skills**—Can he or she source, clean, model, and stage data to subsequently analyze?
- **Analysis skills**—Can he or she describe data through trend and distribution analysis? How about multivariate and other sophisticated statistical analysis?
- **Subject matter expertise**—How well does the analyst understand the dynamics and vagaries of the business domain the data describes?
- **Communication skills**—Can the analyst find and support stories out of the data and analysis? Are these stories tied practically to available options, and do they advance decisions or slow them down?
- **Management skills**—Can the analyst get the job done, on time, on budget? Can he or she lead a team in doing this?
- **Practicality**—Does the analyst demonstrate focus on the decision or action to be informed, and can he or she distinguish "good enough to answer the question" from "perfect"?
- **Curiosity**—Does the analyst generate and test hypotheses beyond what's given?

Developing

Among the interviewees for this book, coincident with the characteristics for which they recruit are efforts to continue developing these skills, both for their teams and for themselves. On-the-job practice applying analytic skills—through multiple, short-cycle repetitions, well-connected to actual execution based on any insights—should be the foundation of any developmental effort. For example, to make sure his analysts understood the realities of the contexts their insights would inform, Harrah's David Norton created a rotation program through which they would be embedded in frontline casino operations for six months.

But beyond hands-on practice, where do analytic leaders turn for ideas? Bed Bath & Beyond's Melanie Murphy says, "I don't read analytics books; I try to read books focused on leadership!" One title she's found useful is Tom Davenport's *Competing On Analytics*, especially for the way it positions the capability she manages as a differentiating asset that senior executives should cultivate, rather than the cost center it's traditionally perceived to be. Talbots' Rob Schmults says, "If I want to learn about something new, I'll root around to find someone who's trying it too, and call them up! The verbal exchange is usually the most efficient for getting to the heart of it. Plus you can get lessons learned and pitfalls to watch out for that you won't read anywhere or hear on a stage." That's an unusually extroverted instinct for many analysts, so any development program you construct might usefully weave in attending a few conferences, and refuse to reimburse dinner for anyone who doesn't come home with at least two business cards, along with thorough trip reports of what's been learned. Or, you can reward the most cards, best write-up, and so on, depending on your motivational inclinations.

Organizing for Analytics

Probably the most common question I hear from executives trying to build their analytics capabilities is "How should we organize for this?" Subsidiary questions include:

- How much do we centralize this function and have it serve multiple business units and functions, versus pushing it into each group?

- What belongs in "the business" versus in IT?

- When and how should we combine "marketing and sales analytics" with "business reporting"?

- Speaking of reporting, to what degree should supplying ongoing reports be combined with analytics groups?

- What degree of integration should I have among my research, analytics, and testing groups?

- What should I try to do in-house, and what should I ask external partners to do for us?

Of course, there are many ways different organizations have answered these questions, and the answers they come to are influenced by a number of factors, including:

- The analytic needs of the business (finding new ways of competing in a choppy and strategically uncertain context, versus riding a successful horse as long and as efficiently as possible)

- Where in a particular technology wave the firm finds itself, and the attendant supply / demand dynamics of that particular phase

- Where a firm is physically located, as this affects its ability to find and attract people with different skills

- The individual skills of its people, as sometimes it makes sense to centralize and share a small but strong analyst cadre, while in other situations it makes sense to push analytic support to talented managers operating at the front edges of the business

- The relative leverage from different analytic approaches at various points

- Factors relating to how effectively insights can be communicated and absorbed across the firm, including distance, language, and culture

Even controlling for these differences in circumstances, the answers appear to be less black and white, and more a matter of degree. The problem is that most organizations don't do nuance very well.

There is a different way to answer questions of organizational structure. It starts with facing and taking advantage of two realities. First, each business opportunity may require different analytic skills, or at least different blends of ones you have. So, the optimal organizational structure may be situation-specific. Second, the circumstances discussed above change, and with them changes your organizational answer. Your killer drug goes off patent. You expand into a new country. It finally really is the Year Of Mobile. Doug Cutting and Mike Cafarella write Hadoop, and Nate Silver joins your summer intern program.

Of course you try to keep an eye on all these changing circumstances. But looking at "input drivers" alone would crush you with its scope and complexity. A second way, then, to manage organization is to track outputs as well as inputs, by looking at the rate at which valuable insights are identified, proven, and scaled by the whole organization. In our work with clients, we begin by grouping demand generation challenges and opportunities into a portfolio, which we mine in quarterly cycles for "3-2-1" results—notionally, in any quarter, our work needs to yield three fresh "news you can use" insights, two real-world tests of these or prior insights, and one idea that's promoted to "production." (The quantities are arbitrary; they're not a bad place to start, but your circumstances may dictate that they be lower initially and higher once you gather steam.)

There are three crucially different characteristics of this approach. One is the integration of the idea that insights need to be not just generated, but tested and scaled as well. Putting these metrics alongside pure insight generation at the heart of the program helps connect analysts to operators. Second is the relatively short timetable (a quarter) for inquiry. As we discuss in Chapter 13, "Culturelytics—A Practical Formula for Change," cultures are collections of values, and values are generalized from observations of successes, failures, and their causes. If you want to improve results and believe that changing culture is part of that, you need to accelerate the rate of observations off which values and cultures change. Also, by doing that, one side benefit is that you take the pressure off any particular change you make to be The One. The third distinguishing feature is its focus on continuous improvement, even as the rate of that improvement may fluctuate. Yes, you may have benchmarked and established goals in the context of customer needs, competitive performance, and necessary returns for the business, but whether you're near or far from those goals is less important than progress toward them. Imperfect, temporary organizational changes that make you better are more valuable than stalling outputs while you perfect structure. (We explore these issues and approaches further in Part III.)

Our executives' experiences and preferences for organizational structures demonstrate this diversity. Doug Collier, CMO at La-Z-Boy, has IT reporting to him, and outsources (for now) marketing mix models and attribution analysis to MarketShare Partners. Rob Schmults at Talbots prefers to insource analytics; in his experience, getting it from media partners produces narrow answers or, worst case, biased ones. Judah Phillips and Melanie Murphy believe strongly in centralizing the analytics function. Paul Magill at Abbott and David Norton at Harrah's created highly matrixed models with significant accountability to and direction from "the field." Mo Chaara's Corporate Analytics Group at Lenovo represents an effort to drive some critical mass for specialized expertise from the center, even as significant analytic capabilities remain aligned with and reside in different business units there. Belinda Lang's experiences at American Express included running a "business interface group" in the IT organization that leveraged fifty statisticians to provide valuable services, but still needed to bridge cultural differences across organizations to be effective, despite Belinda's considerable personal credibility and extensive relationships.

But look more closely. In Doug Collier's case, organization is partly a function of his significant knowledge of and comfort with IT. His CEO is more comfortable having him own it, and IT is comfortable taking direction from him. Rob Schmults, who if not a father of ecommerce was in the room when it was born, is better equipped than the average client partner at a media agency or modeling firm to evaluate the results of an investigation. Judah Phillips and Melanie Murphy are both serious subject matter experts, whose skills and experiences serve not only as management for their analysts but as the fulcrums for strategic alignment and objective decision making in their firms; with strong capable leadership available from them, there's significant leverage to a centralized model. Paul Magill and David Norton had to wrangle central leverage in highly decentralized firms where real power lay in the hands of the country manager or each casino's boss. In every case, each of their solutions was a compromise between vision and reality that allowed each them to build momentum toward the visions and goals their firms had.

Some discussion questions:

- Are your people consistently able to answer the analytic questions that are put to them?
- If not, why?
  - What skill deficiency comes up?
  - What organizational barriers emerge?

- What's your informal networking plan for shaping roles and generating leads related to skill deficiencies?
  - Which social networks and conferences will you invest time and funds in?
- If you're thinking about adjusting your organizational model to overcome a barrier, is your analytic leadership up to the challenge of managing through the change and beyond?

Part II
Practical Analytics: Proven Techniques and Heuristics

5

Practical Frameworks—
For Getting On the Same Page

In Chapter 1, "Strategic Alignment—First You Need to Agree On What to Ask," we explored different attitudinal and functional "fault lines" you might need to manage across to get the strategic alignment necessary to properly build and focus your analytic capabilities. In this chapter, we'll look at ways of packaging your analytic approach for maximum impact. We'll start by describing an artifact I call the "Analytic Brief," which we use in our business, and we'll explore different ways of framing approaches that our interviewees have used successfully.

The Analytic Brief

The Analytic Brief, which I also described in *Pragmalytics*, is so-named as a "riff" on the creative briefs that typically are written to guide advertising and marketing campaigns. Usually, there's been a significant chasm between strategic and budget plans used to obtain funding for such campaigns, and the creative briefs used to inform and shape them. Also, how such campaigns will be evaluated has been more of an afterthought in these documents. Historically, with less flexible and accountable media through which the campaigns would have been realized, this might have been fine. Today it's crucial and possible to evaluate and adjust campaigns on the fly for greatest impact. Accordingly, analytics has to climb into the front seat of the car alongside the initial creative direction for the campaign, with its own plan that was developed parallel to the creative brief. Hence, Analytic Brief.

An Analytic Brief needs to meet three requirements. First, it needs to be comprehensive enough in its reference to different aspects of the business, in terms of function or line of business coverage, to make its various users and influencers feel like their issues can be represented in it. Second, it has to be expressed in a language that is sufficiently plain so as to be clear and universally understood across the range of users. And third, it must be practically "fillable" with data you either have or can readily get so that you can actually apply it (as we discussed in Chapter 2, "Access to Data—Too Often Taken for Granted").

In marketing and sales, for better or for worse, the dominant metaphor for understanding business performance is the "funnel." Descriptions of the stages of the funnel, and of the "paths" that different customers and customer segments take through those stages, vary. The two dominant ways I have observed sales and marketing executives approach a funnel is "top-down/outside-in/experience-driven" versus "bottom-up/inside-out/result-driven." Essentially, the former—representing more the "Venus" perspective from Chapter 1—puts you in the shoes of a customer. It considers his or her needs, starts with how that customer develops awareness of your firm and its products and services, and examines drop-off (the number of customers you lose) at each stage thereafter. The latter—more "Mars"—starts by looking at the business you have (including existing customers and the marketing mix of products and channels), first seeks to maximize the value of those relationships and assets, and then looks incrementally outward from there to find "lookalike" potential customers, using variants of your existing marketing mix more efficiently. (If the planetary metaphor isn't working for you, you can call the former approach a "strategic" approach to the funnel and the latter an "optimization" approach.) The Analytic Brief tries to balance all three perspectives in the questions it encompasses, as the questions invite us to answer them with stories, numbers, and plans equally and iteratively.

Briefly, the Analytic Brief has three levels:

- A "Business Story"
- A "Customer Story"
- A "Test and Learn Plan"

The Business Story lays out relevant customer segments to consider and describes which ones to go after and why. I look for the "why" part to be expressed as a set of quantitatively expressed facts that can be validated or assumptions that can be tested. For example, an auto maker might say, "We're targeting people whose digital habits categorize them as 'luxury car buyers' because we've found that this particular segmentation approach is the most actionable one we've tried, and that prospects we score into this group have a 20% greater lifetime customer value than other 'behavioral clusters' we've been able to practically engineer experiences for."

A Customer Story then articulates a set of needs and a "reference experience" (that is, how the customer wants to navigate, not necessarily how you are currently set up) for the "average" customer in a target segment. Next, it assesses how well your firm's marketing mix maps onto those needs and the reference experience. For example, if suggestions and advice from friends and family through social media channels have become important, it would examine the degree to which your own efforts have kept pace with this trend in terms of investment and attention, and consider how effective your efforts have been. Finally, based on a comparison of how well you're doing across target segments, and across the key needs and experiences they each prefer, you can make decisions about how to shift resources and how to execute differently.

In some cases, the stakes associated with shifting resources and executing differently will be large—for example, the minimum investment level and effort for a television ad can be quite high. Compounding this, you may feel too uncertain about what to do. The data you have may not be sufficient, or your options for action may not have been developed sufficiently for you to pick one. In addition to focusing on relative performance shortfalls at particular experience junctions for key segments, looking for this combination of relatively high stakes and high uncertainty across your options can help you further refine how you invest scarce analytic resources. Finally, you face a choice of how to resolve your uncertainty—whether to talk with customers, examine their past behavior, or set specific tests before them. Collectively, decisions about where and how to look further form the "Test and Learn Plan."

Figure 5.1 presents a graphical, plain-language representation of the Analytic Brief:

The Analytic Brief

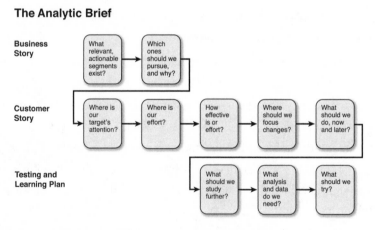

Figure 5.1 The Analytic Brief

Now, let's take the "strategic" perspective one level down. In this case, we'll focus on a target segment's experience. One simple way to "unpack" it is to present it as a table (see Figure 5.2), arraying funnel stages across the top and marketing and sales channels as rows[1]:

Then you can plot dominant channels for each segment at each stage, as well as the "pathways" different customer segments take through your channels as they move through the funnel. There's a lot of debate about whether things are this linear. They may not be, but you have to consider whether the extra nuance you capture is worth the confusion you create by introducing it, at least for alignment purposes.

Here's a way to draw the basics. In Figure 5.3, you simply suggest which channels dominate at each stage for your different target segments (denoted here in red and yellow). Ideally, in addition to color, you add available data to illustrate the relative size of different channels. This could include television viewership based on ratings,

---

[1] This "journey" based representation is not particularly original, but it's widely used. Akin Arikan's excellent book *Multichannel Marketing* (Sybex, 2008) presents one version of it. At Monitor's Marketspace unit, we developed a variant called "Channel Pathways" analysis; one example of its application is described in "The Customer Service Challenge" by Jeffrey Rayport, *Forbes*, December 6, 2005, http://www.forbes.com/2005/12/06/bestbuy-microsoft-hp-cx_jr_1206inmyopinion.html. The refinement we've applied in our work more recently (as shown here) is to flip the funnel on its side to represent a temporal dimension, from left to right. This allows the stages to be varied in length, for a better visual approximation of the overall process. More recently, the "Customer Decision Journey" framework developed by David Edelman at McKinsey & Company has gained some traction due to its better allowance for non-linear processes; Lenovo's Mo Chaara, who I interviewed for this book, indicated it's proven useful there. Judah Phillips offers his version, which he calls "The Tumbler," to describe a mobile-dominated scenario in which shopping, sharing and seeking happen in parallel. My own experience has been that it's better to start with the simplest possible representation to facilitate discussions, and apply more nuanced representations at the firm-specific level once these conversations are underway, than to begin with something too nuanced to be a *lingua franca* at the outset. In 2011, I offered my own metaphor for a "post-funnel" purchase process construct: "The Marketing Funnel is a Brita Water Filter" http://www.octavianworld.org/octavianworld/2011/04/the-marketing-funnel-is-a-brita-water-filter.html.

print circulation, and digital traffic.[2] In Figure 5.4, you suggest the dominant pathway through these channels, for each segment.

Purchase Process

	Attract ⮕	Engage ⮕	Convert ⮕	Retain
Web Site				
Phone				
Search				
Display				
Facebook				
Television				
Stores				
Email				
Twitter				
Smartphone				
Blogs				
Affiliates				
Tablet				

(left axis label: **Channels**)

Figure 5.2   The Purchase Process Grid

---

[2] Here's an example of how you might estimate digital traffic. Let's say you're interested in reaching working age (say, 24–64) male sports fans to sell them equipment. You hypothesize (and, as needed, validate with research) that http://si.com is an important medium for attracting them. Quantcast, a site monitoring service, provides free data on sites that have added its tags to their pages. For example, here's a page profiling si.com: https://www.quantcast.com/si.com?qcLocale=en_US. It reports roughly seven million people per month visiting the site, virtually all men. Compared with the overall age distribution for the U.S. population (as reported here, for example: http://www.censusscope.org/us/chart_age.html), we can see that men in our target age groups "over index" slightly—that is, they are slightly over-represented in the si.com visitor population versus the overall U.S. population. Combining data from the two services, we can estimate that roughly 60% of the site's seven million visitors are in our target group. So, our "Web site/attract" box in the Purchase Process chart would include four million people.

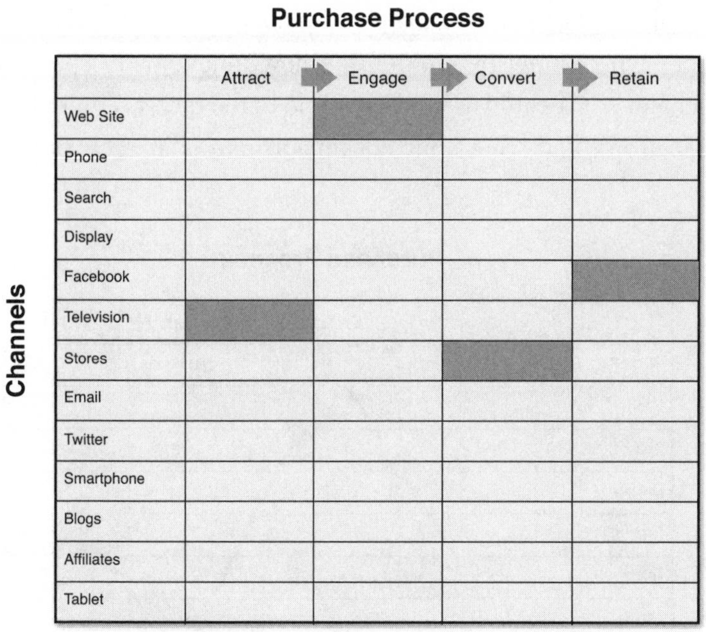
Purchase Process
Attract
Engage
Convert
Retain
Channels
Web Site
Phone
Search
Display
Facebook
Television
Stores
Email
Twitter
Smartphone
Blogs
Affiliates
Tablet

Figure 5.3 The Purchase Process Heat Map

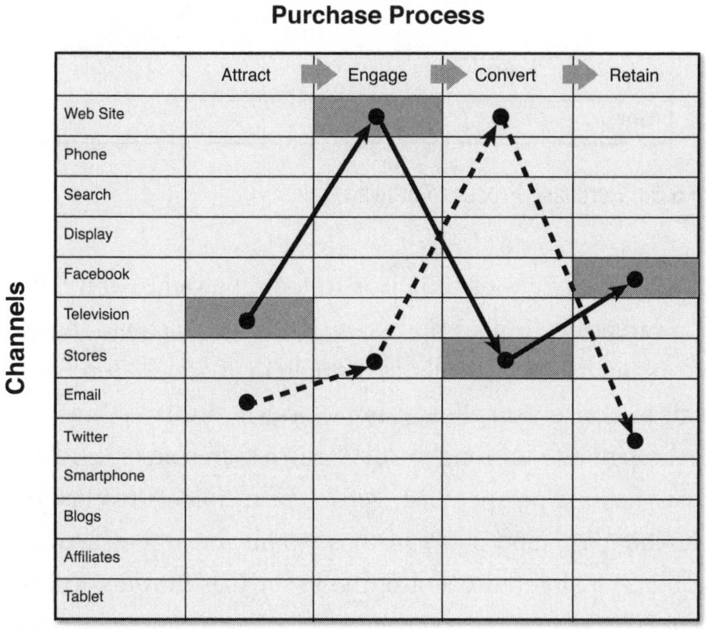
Purchase Process
Attract
Engage
Convert
Retain
Channels
Web Site
Phone
Search
Display
Facebook
Television
Stores
Email
Twitter
Smartphone
Blogs
Affiliates
Tablet

Figure 5.4 Purchase Process Pathways

Finally, as in Figure 5.5, you can evaluate the cost and effectiveness of each channel by considering how much you're spending in each channel (allocated as far as possible to the target segment you're interested in), and what your conversion rate is at each step along the way.

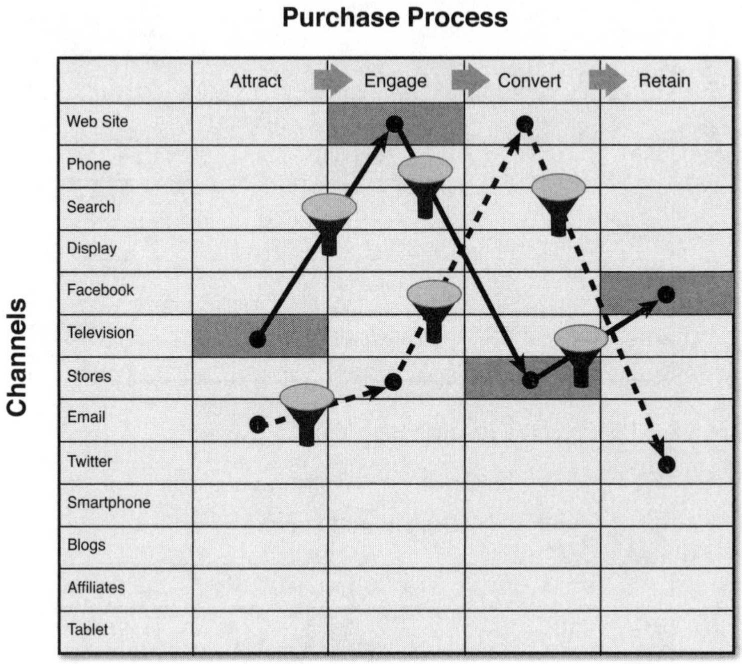

Purchase Process

Figure 5.5   Purchase Process Pathway Yields

One general rule of thumb is to look for yields well below 1% from awareness-raising impressions to call-to-action engagement behaviors, and then typically mid-single-digit yields step to step on through to conversion. For example, run a display ad, see a CTR (click-through rate) of roughly 0.1%; run a search ad or send an email out to a qualified prospect list, get 5% of recipients to click through to a landing page, and 3–5% of those to buy once they arrive. Obviously, the less targeted you are, the lower these results will be, and *vice versa*.

The "optimization" approach ends up looking at the same information (conversion performance and cost) but starts without the "customer experience" narrative to frame it. For example, if you were to ask a marketing manager in banking, "How's business?" one answer you might get would be, "Well, our CPA (cost per acquired customer) is up." If you were to probe further (after adjusting for changes in business conditions and maybe seasonality), you might ask to *de-average* that observation along a few different dimensions: by channels, or perhaps by customer deciles (ranking customers acquired by CPA and breaking the distribution into ten groups, then asking whether the increase in CPA is uniformly or disproportionately concentrated among certain customers). However, you haven't yet started any discussion of a customer "journey" and you might not get to it until you're deep into trying to explain the trends or performance distributions you're seeing.

Figure 5.6, which we call an "Attract-Engage-Convert" chart, provides an example of "de-averaging" in search of optimization opportunities from our own work with retailers. The size of each bubble in the diagram represents the number of unique visitors per month for each retailer. The horizontal axis shows how often, on average, each visitor comes to the retailer's site in each month. The vertical axis shows each retailer's conversion rate—the rate at which each visit, in this case, yields a purchase (not *visitor*-based conversion). One nice feature of including three different metrics on a single display like this is that you can observe and explore the tradeoffs that might come from emphasizing any particular single metric.

Now here's where it gets interesting. If you're de-averaging across channels or content, how do you know how much credit to give to the "converting" or "last touch" point of contact? In recent years, marketers have begun to evolve from simple, heuristic approaches to "attribution analysis" that simply assign all conversion credit to the last touch point, or across them based on simple static rules, and toward much more rigorous, statistically-derived "full attribution" methods that examine how much of the variance in conversion (or any dependent measure of interest) can be assigned to different controllable "variables" (which could be channels, creative executions, offers, and so on). This is done mainly using complex linear regression models that use lots of data. Increasingly, the outputs of this analysis (changes in "fully attributed conversion cost," for example) are automatically integrated with marketing automation platforms that can act on these arbitrage opportunities (as the cooler kids call them). (There's risk in straying from the "simple language" commandment as you introduce tools like this, but it's manageable if you pay attention to it, constantly circling back to jargon- and metaphor-free explanations.)

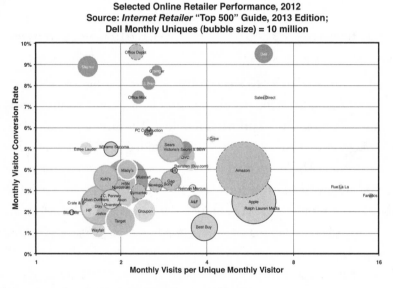

Figure 5.6 Retail Attract-Engage-Convert Chart

Within certain channels, such as digital display advertising, this process has been refined to the point that adjustments to decisions such as "which publisher's available inventory to buy at what price" are made in milliseconds. This practice is known as "real time bidding," or "RTB," and is a subset of "programmatic buying" (a real-time decision to serve an ad to an impression at a pre-fixed price;

the impression can be described by the cookie it's associated with, the contextual characteristics of the associated editorial, or both[3]). It already has a very meaningful share of the display ad market and is projected to command a dominant share in just a few short years.[4]

Industry veterans will observe that what we're calling "attribution modeling" today used to be called "media mix modeling." To understand what has changed, it's important to move past the labels and look at the following factors:

- The frequency of the analysis and of adjustments based on it
- The granularity of the attribution to be done (for example, for one whole channel versus all others, or for different publishers within an channel)
- The scope of channels to be considered, as available channels multiply

Some of you will note parallels with the "velocity, volume, and variety" that Big Data experts use to describe what distinguishes that characterization.[5] Right now, orchestrating the resources necessary to execute full-attribution analysis (let alone execute the necessary integrations to act on its insights) is logistically challenging, and there are significantly increasing returns to scale and experience in meeting these challenges. Few organizations are able to reach the necessary levels of scale and experience to see these returns. So today, a very dynamic industry is growing up around a set of firms, including independents such as Visual IQ and Adometry, and captives such

---

[3] John Ebbert, "Define It: What Is Programmatic Buying?" *Adexchanger*, November 19, 2012, 12:06am http://www.adexchanger.com/online-advertising/define-programmatic-buying/.

[4] "Programmatic Ad Spend Set To Soar," *eMarketer*, October 30, 2013 http://www.emarketer.com/Article/Programmatic-Ad-Spend-Set-To-Soar/1010343.

[5] Diya Soubra, "The 3 V's That Define Big Data," *Data Science Central*, July 5, 2012 5:11am http://www.datasciencecentral.com/forum/topics/the-3vs-that-define-big-data.

as eBay's ClearSaleing, that provide this capability as a hosted, outsourced service.

Each of the two approaches we've discussed has an important place in the senior executive's toolkit. The "strategic approach" provides a wonderful way to tell stories that can help improve alignment across complex organizations and can also be the basis for a roadmap for increasingly sophisticated optimization capabilities. The "optimization" approach, in particular the more sophisticated recent developments in attribution modeling, helps to apply a mathematical rigor to the observations we make about the effectiveness of different channels and other marketing assets. In the end, it pays to work both ends to the middle: Tell stories, but be sure to de-average (and avoid "narrative fallacies," a concept described by Hayden White[6] and further popularized by Nassim Taleb[7]). Optimize! But, beware excessively narrow scopes and the diminishing returns that go with them. Also, as you improve the effectiveness of your execution in different channels, be sure to re-run your models to reflect these enhancements. Or, if data doesn't accumulate fast enough, put your thumb on the scale to credit recent gains in a channel's performance not yet reflected in the data you have.

So how do others cut into articulating the most relevant questions and aligning people around those priorities?

Rob Schmults, who leads ecommerce at Talbot's, the women's clothing retailer, is a fan of the blended approach. "The first thing I do is look *across* the business, both 'customer-experience-in' and 'conversion-data-out.' I use both qualitative and quantitative data to support a higher-level analysis for bigger opportunities," Rob says. The reason he does this is because he often sees a problem in the construction of customer experiences in his world that he calls the "Layer

---

[6] "Hayden White," http://en.wikipedia.org/wiki/Hayden_White.

[7] "The Narrative Fallacy," http://en.wikipedia.org/wiki/The_Black_Swan_ (2007_book)#The_narrative_fallacy.

Cake": a three-tiered, semi-sequential unpacking of the experience into an examination of how well "Acquisition," "Creative" (branding-related), and "Site Mechanics" are working. Acquisition refers to the collection of channels the firm is using to attract demand. These extend to working a house list, to digital advertising—display and search advertising in traditional, social, and mobile channels—as well as to more conventional offline channels. "Creative" refers to how well different messages and executions are working in relevant channels. "Site Mechanics" encompasses the features and functions deployed on owned properties, as well as merchandising decisions. The problem, as Rob sees it, is that a customer is often traveling through an experience that's been crafted by multiple entities, each doing its own thing typically with minimal collaboration (creative, SEM, site operations, site merchandising, CRM, email, and so on). This fragmentation is often compounded by decisions to execute some experience elements in-house and others with third-party vendors. After many years in the world of ecommerce, Rob has a sense for how, quantitatively, different techniques should perform across a customer experience in his sector, and how to adjust his efforts accordingly. But he's also got an attribution modeling capability in place to crosscheck his observations. (See Part IV, "Conversations with Practitioners," for more detail about how Rob makes these adjustments.)

For Scott McDonald, who leads the research function at Condé Nast, insights have historically come from studying distributions around mean conversion rates carefully. Over- or under-spending on any particular decile on a list of potential subscribers because you have misread their propensity to convert can be very expensive, in both direct and opportunity costs. Looking for subtle changes in results across multiple dimensions, to find variables that better explain those shifts, such as the aging of a magazine's readership or the frequency of solicitations, remains a continuous part of a constant search for more efficiency.

Scott's opportunity and challenge are both compounded today by the advent of digital channels. In theory, observing subscribers' behavior online should allow better tuning of renewal offers, both online and off. Unfortunately, the cookies we use to track folks get deleted at a pretty good clip (the going rate appears to be a 30% per month deletion rate). Also, it's not always easy to track people across laptops, tablets, and phones, and there's still not as much overlap between print and digital readers as you might think. Nonetheless, while it's hard to be 100% certain whom you're targeting, Scott and his colleagues, through a variety of mechanisms described in the interview in Part IV, use these online behaviors as independent variables in models that help them better describe their audiences, predict their responses *probabilistically* to different offers, and adjust marketing efforts accordingly.

Doug Collier, CMO of furniture maker La-Z-Boy Incorporated and President of its international division, described to me how the firm's manufacturing comeback informed the marketing side of the business. At one point following the 2008 crash, things were pretty dire, and the firm needed to cut up to 25% of its costs in some areas within 90 days to survive. It did so, and the discipline it used to make the necessary changes extended into the adoption of tools like 6-Sigma, Kaizen, and 5S[8], all of which depend on a process-oriented, data-driven, simplicity-emphasizing, experimentally-guided approach to evolving operations. This created a competitive pressure for marketing. As Doug says, "Manufacturing upped its game, and we needed to as well!" Today, much of marketing's analytic approach reflects these philosophies; in particular, testing has become foundational.

Overall, the dominant point-of-departure perspective today for marketing analytics appears to be the Venusian one. Mo Chaara notes that McKinsey's Customer Decision Journey model is popular at

---

[8] "5S (Methodology)," http://en.wikipedia.org/wiki/5S_(methodology).

Lenovo. Melanie Murphy reports productive application of "personas" and "use cases" in her experiences. Annemarie Frank describes how a Customer Experience perspective has been brought to bear at HSN to better frame ongoing optimization in the context of the full value of a customer relationship, rather than individual transactions. But full-attribution-based optimization follows close behind, as more organizations figure out the first few steps of the roadmap for that value journey.

Some discussion questions:

- What frameworks are popular in your firm?
- Why are they popular?
    - Latest business book?
    - Past successful experience applying them?
- Are they appropriate to the issues being addressed?
- How memorable and portable are they? Are they understood in common within the analytic organization and across its borders with operators?

6

Practical Research—Beyond Studies for Studies' Sake

Historically, marketing channels in particular generated little data directly. You couldn't really tell how many people actually watched, heard, read, or passed by an ad, so primary research became the first dominant analytic discipline for the marketing function. This research mostly asked people about their exposure to and experiences with advertising and marketing, current or planned, through small focus groups and larger surveys. If customer behaviors were directly observed, in real time or, say, through recordings, samples for these direct behaviors tended to be small, episodic, and inconsistent in design.

Since some data is better than none, things operated this way for quite some time. An enormous momentum grew up behind this approach, in the forms of an industry providing these services, in-house departments purchasing these services and reporting their findings, and academics teaching future practitioners. Sophisticated surveying and statistical techniques—randomizing the order of questions, weighting the answers of certain kinds of respondents—were applied to massage samples so they would approximate as closely as possible the characteristics of the underlying populations being studied. At its very best, the research discipline has provided highly accurate predictive power. Nate Silver's meta-analysis of multiple political polls, which evaluated and adjusted for known biases in each poll, was a perfect 50 for 50 in predicting how each state would vote in the last presidential election.

Gathering data this way has traditionally been very expensive.[1] This has led to cutting corners in more or less visible ways that compromise its value. Samples are trimmed beyond the point of any appropriate confidence levels and intervals, or research vendors present cuts of subgroups without clear reference to the loss of statistical explanatory power. Surveys are designed by less experienced hands that, for example, don't balance open-ended and closed-ended questions appropriately, or forget to randomize the order of answer options to control for bias. Weighting schemes that attempt to compensate for sampling shortcomings get too cute by half and collapse under their own weight when, at the first probe by an ultimate consumer of the information, they can't be explained in plain English.

All these potential flaws are piled on top of two inescapable shortcomings of primary research. First, what people say doesn't often match well to what they actually do, and a rational response can't always predict an emotional reaction. Sometimes this bias is unconscious, and sometimes it represents an active filter: "What does this person want to hear? If I'm honest will I be embarrassed? Will the answer trigger additional questions I don't have time for?" Second, the answers you get can be especially influenced by how you recruit your sample, in ways that might be hidden from statisticians subsequently trying to adjust for sampling bias, for example by different motivations for responding (for example, belief in the cause, or compensation). (To be fair, research to date has been inconclusive to sanguine on the effects of compensation in general. Eleanor Singer at the University of Michigan, in a review of the literature, writes, "We have found no studies of the effect of incentives on the validity or reliability

---

[1] This is changing with the advent of web-mediated research, as exemplified by services like Google Survey: http://www.google.com/insights/consumersurveys/home.

of answers, and this [*sic*] aspect of quality is an important research question."[2])

And so, with primary research, you have three tasks. The first is to make sure you're applying it to the right questions. In general, primary research will be more useful today for understanding the *why* behind the *what* that can increasingly be tracked through other means. Traditionally, research follows a "qual-then-quant" process; conversations through focus groups and small surveys help inform hypotheses that are then researched and reported quantitatively through larger-sample, follow-on, closed-ended surveys. Today, with more channel-generated data available to suggest hypotheses—for example, that people are seeing a firm's ads—that can be validated quantitatively, research can be focused to better explain what's going on when looking at the channel-generated data that generates a lot of "correlation is not causality" doubt. For example, research might help address a scenario like, "People who see our location-based advertising on their smartphones then walk into our stores. But were they influenced by the ads, or were they going to our store anyway?"

Second, you need to vet research thoroughly. Make sure you understand how the sample was recruited and how its profile compares with the profile of the underlying population. Make sure you match the confidence levels and intervals the sample makes possible to the stakes of any decisions informed by your research. Make sure you understand any weights or other adjustments applied to groups within the sample. Make sure you go through the questions asked, and that you are comfortable that they not only match the substance you're after, but that they don't introduce inappropriate biases (or, if they do, that you are controlling them as much as possible). The Pew Research Center website's Methodology section provides a very good

---

[2] Singer, Eleanor, "The Use of Incentives to Reduce Nonresponse in Household Surveys," p. 9, http://www.isr.umich.edu/src/smp/electronic%20copies/51-draft106.pdf.

model you might follow for issues that must be addressed, as well as how that particular organization has resolved those issues.[3]

The third task is to know the limits of research, when and how to substitute or complement research with analytics (data recording engagement and purchase interactions), and testing. When your past data is very dirty, limited, or incomplete, testing is logistically hard to organize, and assembling a sample is straightforward and inexpensive, addressing the marginal question through research can be highly productive. Further, when the specific behavior you're interested in can be closely isolated without sacrificing relevance, research can be more accurate and revealing. For example, asking, "When you shop, what factors are most important to you?" is very different than asking, "When you bought that sweater last Tuesday, what factor(s) converted you from a shopper to a buyer?" But as the state of your data is better, the cost and complexity of testing is cheaper, and the relevance of specific behaviors to probe for declines, so too will the relative utility of research begin to diminish.

There are ways you can make this a constructive dynamic within your analytic organization, rather than a zero-sum struggle for resources and airtime. Position the balance of research resources as close to field marketing and sales groups as possible, with a lean center to provide cross-business brand tracking and tactical research support. Crosscheck all your disciplines' output constantly. Is a research finding consistent with what our data tell us? Are either or both corroborated by a test result? Keep your base level of ongoing *what*-related research lean, relying as much as possible on syndicated (and thus less expensive) services; as Doug Collier does at La-Z-Boy, keep your powder dry for *why* investigations. Finally, while the *zeitgeist* has "data" in the ascendant, treat all your disciplines as equal, complementary partners, whose primary value comes from their role as

---

[3] "Methodology," Pew Research Center for the People and the Press, http://www. people-press.org/methodology/.

business problem solvers, for which their technical skills are means to an end.

Some discussion questions:

- To what degree do you have research playing the right role in your analytic mix?
- If research is overused or underused, is it because of a lack or surplus of experience or confidence in other approaches? Or, is it a matter of convenience?
- To what degree have you crosschecked the findings from your research with findings from analytics and testing?
- If people you survey are telling you one thing, and your observation of their behavior through analysis or testing suggests another, what's behind this mismatch?

7

Practical Analytics—Knowing When to Say When

All analytic challenges come with stakes associated with the decisions to be made, and with implicit time and resource constraints. The more clearly these are applied to managing the analytic effort, the more productive and successful your analytic function will be. This chapter suggests some specific techniques that can be used to wring the value from analytic efforts appropriate to the decision to be made, under these constraints.

Evaluating Performance

Let's assume you have used all three "Venus," "Mars," and "Earth" approaches we described in Chapter 1, "Strategic Alignment—First You Need to Agree On What to Ask," to generate a list of marketing and sales resources or program elements to shift resources to and from. How do you assess their performance to inform your eventual judgments? Numbers (for example, a conversion rate) in isolation mean nothing—they need to be compared.

There are five kinds of comparisons you can make. The first three don't require a perfect apples-to-apples comparison; rather, what you're trying to do is divine a relative sense of urgency.

1. You can look at trends in different relevant metrics. How much change has there been? How steep is the change? How "noisy" is the trend? Is it speeding up or slowing down? If you've seen rapid advances but now diminishing gains in improving conversion rates, for example, it might be time to shift your attention to direct channels for acquiring new leads or even brand-building activities.

2. You can "de-average" a number and look "within" it to identify hidden issues demanding attention. What does the distribution look like if you cut it by certain important dimensions? For example, slice your average order value by product category or by customer segment. Does this lead you to possible shifts in your merchandising plans or to your loyalty program?

3. If your analysis is based on a sample, what if any biases exist in the sample, or in the distribution of the underlying data the sample is drawn from, that you need to adjust for? For example, do you need to weight the responses of certain survey respondents you sample to match the proportions of the groups in the underlying population these respondents represent?

4. You can benchmark the number externally. Taken singly, most benchmarks you want are either unavailable or suspect if they are there. But you can do better if, like an experienced entrepreneur approaches recruiting, you approach benchmarking as a continuous process. You're always on the hunt for points of comparison, assessing them not for perfection but perhaps improvement over what you've had before and applying a "look but don't stare" perspective on your own performance in their context (for example, by comparing trends). Every good sector-specific analyst I know has a sense of normal ranges for vital signs of the business composed of individual performance benchmarks that tells him or her whether something's out of whack (for example, in ecommerce, *Internet Retailer*'s "Top 500" guide is full of useful information; for email marketers,

emailstatcenter.com is also a terrific source of help). This sense is gained through experience but can be accelerated through formal and informal research and networking.

5. You can drive for an "exchange rate" across different relevant metrics. This has two components. The first is to pick what the reference "common currency" will be. Rob Schmults, for example, advocates using an eCPA, or "effective Cost Per Acquisition" in his business. The second is to properly credit different channels and messages for their roles in influencing customers to the desired end. This is called "attribution." Annemarie Frank at HSN describes how her firm is pushing even further, simultaneously moving from last-click to "full" attribution (on a measured timetable), while also moving toward a better "Mars-Venus" balance between a transactional orientation (how many sales did this product or promotion get, what are sales per minute of network time) and a relationship perspective which looks at customer lifetime value and evaluates engagement investments, such as games or events, in that context.

Aside: Attribution Analysis

There are three approaches you can take to the attribution analysis we briefly described. The first two are simple and useful if you're just getting started. One is to ignore spreading the credit and simply give full credit to the "last click," or to the channel through which the final purchase comes (say, a search ad or your call center). Another is to apply arbitrary credit amounts to different channels. So, for example, let's say you have two acquisition channels—TV ads and paid search ads. Let's also say that you have one conversion channel, your web site, and that 100% of its traffic comes through your paid search ads. You spend $100 on TV ads and $100 on paid search, and you made 20 sales in the relevant period. If you give no credit to TV ads, your eCPA for that channel is infinite, and you just continue to spend on it "because it's the right thing to do." Your eCPA for paid search is \$100/20, or \$5. If you decide, arbitrarily, that half the sales that came through paid search are fully influenced through TV, and the paid search ad is simply a navigation convenience (effectively part of the conversion channel along with your web site), then half the sales go to TV, and each channel's eCPA is \$100/10, or \$10.

The third way to do attribution involves looking backward to understand how changes in investments in different channels are correlated, and then using this information to calculate appropriate attributions. So for (a very simple) example, if you notice that roughly 25% of the variance in your paid-search-sourced website traffic can be explained by changes in your TV spend, you might decide that TV ads influence a quarter of your website traffic (again, for simplicity, all coming through paid search). Accordingly, your eCPA for TV would be \$100/5, or \$20. (Of course you might also decide that your TV spend "reinforces your brand," and thus influences sales in future periods, and adjust your math accordingly. Modeling pros call this "ad-stocking," and there's a whole subfield of marketing analytics art and science around how to do this.)

Now take this to its logical extreme. Envision a statistical analysis—specifically, a complex multivariate regression—in which you assess the relationship between of all your different touch points, down to the very granular level of different publishers, partners, and creative variants, on the one hand, and a set of business objectives (eCPA, for example) on the other. Next, imagine updating this model as regularly as the data sets behind these touch points refresh themselves. Then think of training the machines to refine the model(s) automatically, for better fit and predictive power. Finally, envision automating the connection between predictions and decisions, so that the trades we described earlier (sell this channel/publisher/creative, buy that one) are also made automatically, as far as possible. This is where, as of this writing, the envelope of possibility currently lies—and there's a healthy amount of activity there[1], as my conversation with Ben Clark, Wayfair's senior architect for the firm's product search and recommendation services, suggests. But as you probably can guess, you can't get there overnight. Given the state of your data, and the collective capabilities and inclinations of your people and organizations, how you plot and execute the path from here to there matters as much, or more, as the final vision.

Do the Math

All analytic opportunities come with an "envelope of economic possibility" that governs how much it's worth spending on them. This envelope typically emerges from the initial observations that motivate the analysis. For example, let's say you're a sales manager, and you notice that your sales cycle—the time it takes from an initial lead to a closed sale—has doubled. The relevant analytic questions are "Why is this happening?" and "What can we, and what should we, do about it?"

The relevant math for this might be something like, "At the extreme, if it takes twice as long to close sales, and our close rate doesn't change, then there's a risk that our sales for upcoming period X would be one third lower." Table 7.1 illustrates this effect:

---

[1] I'm grateful to my friends Manu Mathew and Anto Chittilappilly, the founders of Visual IQ (http://visualiq.com), the leading multi-channel attribution firm in the industry, for teaching me about this. Anything I get right I owe to them, and any errors are, of course, mine.

Table 7.1   Effects of a Lengthening Sales Cycle

	P1	P2	P3	P4	Total
Old Reality					
Leads	10	10	10	10	
Sales		2	2	2	6
New Reality: sales cycle is twice as long; lead generation and close rates unchanged					
Leads	10	10	10	10	
Sales			2	2	4

Let's say each sale is worth $20,000. Let's assume the marginal profit contribution on each sale is 50%, or $10,000. Two fewer sales during the period would mean $20,000 less collected. How much can you afford to spend to identify the reasons behind this problem? This question poses a bit of a dilemma. Without knowing the causes, it's hard to know solutions and thus the costs of those solutions. Without knowing those costs, it's hard to budget for the analysis to uncover the causes.

Proceed Iteratively

When I worked at Bain & Company, the strategy consulting firm, case teams I worked with adapted the hypothesis-driven problem solving approach the firm used by adding what we called an "answer slam" (which I previously described in *Pragmalytics*). The idea was to try to see if we could start by answering the questions posed above ("What's going on?" "What can/should we do about it?") in just a few minutes. Then, based on how satisfied we were with the answers, we would decide whether we should spend a day, and then a week, and so forth, to refine the overall answer (or particular elements of it). By doing this, we worked both ends of the dilemma posed above to the middle. We developed an early sense of what causes and options might be, and we estimated potential costs. At the same time, we got a sense for where our conclusions might lie, how much uncertainty there was about them, and how hard it was going to be to resolve that uncertainty. Contrast this with a more conventional approach to analysis in which the work of answering these questions would start, passively, with "OK, what's your budget for this work, and by when do you need an answer?" From there, work would fill the time and resources available to it, and proceed in a relatively silo-ed fashion: one person on the team would run one subset of questions to ground, while a second tackled a different set, with global optimization of the team's time rolled up to the team manager level—or even higher, in the case of more complex analytic challenges. This is fine if review cycles are kept inside the "turning circle" of the overall project (as was the case at Bain), but in many firms' in-house analytic groups, team meetings tend to be more about status and process issues than about the work itself, and so opportunities for these kinds of in-flight adjustments are often missed.

Interpolate Estimates

In the world of Big Data, the big breakthrough of recent years has been software that allows you to harness multiple cheap processors together to take a massive computing task and use parallel processing on a massive scale to execute it. The traditional approach would have been to try to scale proprietary database software on bigger and bigger individual machines. The sizes and processing intensities of the relevant data sets made this latter approach exponentially more expensive to pursue with the traditional approach. With the new approach, software costs (even free software must be properly configured) are much lower, and hardware (processors and storage) can be scaled more linearly.

The same metaphor applies in the world of analytics, whether looking at past data, conducting research, or pursuing tests. Let's say you're interested in better reading the impact of brand-level investments on metrics such as unaided awareness or consideration. One traditional approach is to conduct a brand study. If you are relying on just this one source and you're making this assessment once a year, you will probably beef up your sample size. Since you're running it once a year, your survey might be longer, and thus you'd have to contact more people in order to get enough respondents to yield the target sample size. Since your machinery has to ramp up annually, as opposed to being tuned to run continuously with maximum efficiency, that larger sample will cost disproportionately more to gather.

A different approach combines two different elements. One is to sample more regularly, using less expensive syndicated research. Strictly speaking, and especially if your business is seasonal, measuring these factors at different points during the year might give you somewhat different answers to the same questions, but over the course of the year you would begin to approximate the sample size of the annual survey, and you would learn whether in fact there was some sort of seasonal movement in the metrics. The net result would be more insight at less cost.

The second element of this approach is to supplement your direct measurement of unaided awareness and consideration with "Platonic Shadow" metrics. These are proxies for the truth that, while not perfect reads on the matter at hand, are close enough to be relevant and useful. One good example is searching for patterns in searches for your firm's name on Google Trends[2], perhaps comparing it with your category and/or relevant competitors. This is a tool we've used successfully for several years now in our work. Others, including digital analytics guru Avinash Kaushik[3], have also described its use for this purpose in great detail, including specific suggestions for how it can

---

[2] "Google Trends," http://www.google.com/trends/.

[3] Avinash Kaushik, "Excellent Analytics Tip #20: Measuring Digital "Brand Strength," *Occam's Razor*, http://www.kaushik.net/avinash/analytics-measuring-digital-brand-strength/.

help you geo-target advertising investments. Of course this works best if your target audience is consumers who use search in their purchasing process. But if you are after a narrower audience, you can use your own website traffic—particularly direct traffic, and to a slightly lesser degree traffic referred from organic search—as proxies.

All these sources of information are free and can be useful cross-checks of what your primary brand research tools are telling you. If you see convergence in the answers across the data sets, you're improving your confidence in what your investment in the primary research is telling you. If the numbers point in different directions, it could be a clue that you need to dig in a bit further.

Model Iteratively

Many analytic organizations include a reporting group that organizes data and builds and maintains dashboards over it, and then analytic groups that do *ad hoc,* deep-dive, custom analysis into this data. The latter group typically gets populated with the "more capable and experienced" analysts—so the task of building models to explain and predict patterns and relationships in the data falls to them. Because they are more capable and experienced, and because they are a) more fluent in modeling and b) concerned that they need to prove their mastery of complexity to perpetuate their exalted status, the models they build more often than not tend to start with too much complexity. This is done with the best intentions: to squeeze out as much explanatory power as possible.

In our work, we have occasionally inherited complex models executed as episodic investigations into past relationships, and we then worked to transform them into predictive tools that are "operationalized"—or, simplified as far as practically feasible without compromising their explanatory and predictive powers, in order to make them less expensive to refresh regularly (since tapping, cleaning, and transforming data can be expensive). In one case, we started with a model that had more than two dozen variables and narrowed it down to a handful, while only losing 1% of the variation explained by the model.

A different and better approach is to build models up from simplicity instead of down from complexity. Every time we juxtapose time series of two variables, we are implicitly creating conclusions about their relationship that effectively constitute a model. Browsing for good fits, and perhaps adding a lag factor as needed, can often yield one or two variables that each account for 10 to 30% of the variation in the dependent variable.

To be clear, this is not a Luddite screed arguing against complex models. The work of Ben Clark's team at Wayfair is an illustration of sophisticated models that not only provide superior predictive power, but that do so cost-effectively. In Wayfair's case, however, this sophistication has emerged out of a set of well-managed, ecosystemic conditions, and they did things more simply before things got more complicated. And so at Wayfair, this capability literally is part of the furniture, instead of being at risk of bouncing off the atmosphere as happens in so many other places.

Assessing Solution Tradeoffs

At this point you have applied "Venus," "Mars," and "Earth" perspectives, and you have zeroed in on a number of potential needs or identified opportunities. You have assigned a relative **value** to each. Further, you've "done the math" as far as possible to convert these assessments to some absolute measure of value (incremental sales, profits) and perhaps even discounted them to a net present value to make them even more comparable. For example, you might say, "If we were able to increase our conversion rate from 1% to 1.25%, that would mean an incremental x sales, with an average order value (AOV) of $y, for $z extra revenue. At our average margin, that would be worth another $a in profits; discounting that back over the next two to three years would be worth $b." Or, you might say, "The differences in fully-attributed eCPA between our least expensive and most expensive channels suggest we could move $x million from the latter to the former and increase our sales by y percent at no additional cost. This would generate $z marginal contribution per year, and so on."

Now you need to assess the relative **feasibility** of tackling these different opportunities. Ideally, of course, you develop budgets and schedules, but these take time and investment themselves, and you may not want to green-light their development until you have a general sense of whether related initiatives might move ahead. You can, however, triage them on the feasibility dimension using some simple rules of thumb suggested by the experiences of our interviewees:

- If you control the means through which actions based on insights would be taken—that is, you control access to data for insights, and associated media budgets or execution channels, such as an email marketing system—then feasibility is highest.

- If you must partner across the organization in ways that have not already been established, or if you must integrate data sources *within* the control of the organization that you have not previously worked with to gain new insights, then feasibility is moderate.

- Finally, if you have to bring in a new resource that requires coordinating multiple functions within your organization beyond the ones you directly control—say, purchase and implement a new marketing automation platform within your IT infrastructure—feasibility is lowest. This extends even to offerings packaged as services, where you need to provide data to outside vendors; the logistics for contracting and supporting are often deceptively complex and time-consuming.

Now you're ready to compare your options for solutions. Rob Schmults uses a simple plot of value versus "do-ability" (which carries a slightly different meaning for him, as distinguished from feasibility: "It's not can it be done, but rather, can *we*, practically-speaking, get it done?"). As he manages them, these assessments are not done by analytic teams in isolation but rather in close consultation within his function and with related partners (IT, for example). These assessments are then packaged for review, by senior executive committees who allocate funding on the annual budgeting cycle and periodic re-budgeting adjustment intervals.

Some discussion questions:

- How well-suited do you feel your analytic efforts are to the decisions you are supporting?
- Too superficial?
    - About right, in terms of complexity and sophistication?
    - Too complex, over-done?
- If your efforts are misaligned to the decisions being taken, what's behind that?
    - Too much or too little sophistication?
    - Too much or too little conservatism?

8

Practical Testing—An Underused Approach to Insight

A few years ago, a very wise client of mine said, "Cesar, you have to remember that in the end every marketing program we do is a test, whether we set it up formally that way or not. What's important is whether you are open to learning from the result."

For me this was a profoundly important insight. I, along with many others, had fallen into the trap of thinking conventionally about testing as a phase between design and implementation, or as a capability that you bolted on after you had set up your basic infrastructure for ongoing execution. Or, worse: it's not uncommon to hear a mid-level marketing manager say words to the effect of, "We're too busy executing the program to measure and test it!"

The scope of testing we'll discuss here is broad. Most readers will think of testing in the context of digital media (for example, email, web pages, display ads), such as A/B testing (in which entirely separate pages are shown) or multivariate tests (in which components of a single page are varied, with tracking of the relative effectiveness of those combinations of variants). Many of course will think of focus groups, or "matched market" tests of traditional advertising. Still others might think of varying scripts in call centers.

One of the most important obstacles to expanding testing programs is the need to provide for a control group. A common objection to testing revolves around the lack of infrastructure, particularly in inbound channels like websites, for administering a solid control. For example, someone might say that if you're not randomizing exposures at each request of a web page, and rather showing one version "A" on a Monday and the other "B" on a Tuesday, Tuesday's lift over Monday might not be due to the superiority of "B" but rather to Tuesday-related factors. One simple thing you can do in cases like this is to review past differences in performance across attributes (in this case "day of week") and shrink Tuesday's lift by a factor that reflects any past differences you see. This is analogous to "seasonally adjusting" economic statistics, for example.

In outbound channels, if your infrastructure doesn't automate things for you, you can split-test manually. If you are sending out an email, for example, you can randomly split your list in half—send out version "A" of your message at 10:00 a.m. and then version "B" of your message at 10:01 a.m. If you are running a television campaign, you can run your test and control cells in "matched markets," or markets that share the properties of your target customers. Note that in this case, you need to make sure you're not just matching for their demographic characteristics, but also for behavioral and attitudinal factors that might be relevant to you, such as whether you've seen a minimum amount of web traffic (as a proportion of population) from matched market candidates, or whether (more conventionally) their brand development index versus category development index scores are similar.[1]

There are at least two different ways of thinking about how you deploy testing. One is the notion of a test as a regular but episodic thing you do on the road to picking a "winner" that will then get deployed 100% of the time. Another is to use a "champion/challenger" model, where, say, 90% of the "exposures" in deployment or production go to a "champion" variant that performed best

---

[1] "Brand Development Index," http://en.wikipedia.org/wiki/Brand_Development_Index.

initially, but 10% go to a pool of challengers that is regularly refreshed to see if a successor to the extant champion can be found. As a general rule, the latter is preferable if you can sustain it logistically, because it allows you to observe whether your test results are consistent or whether they regress toward the mean over time. Alternatively, you can set thresholds for how much better a challenger must be to justify relevant switching costs.

It's very easy to lose momentum in a testing program—to let it become optional. In my experience, there are two ways to reinforce testing. One is to calendar it: create a "test of the week" program with a "field date" and a "review date." Another is, when senior executives ask you, "How can I help you be more successful?" after one of your analytic presentations, to ask *them* to ask, "What tests have we conducted this month, and what have we learned from them?" At every opportunity, especially at their staff meetings, ask them to reinforce testing.

Some discussion questions:

- How significant a part of your analytic arsenal is testing?
    1. "We test rarely, if at all—we study carefully, and then execute monolithically."
    2. "We test as part of informing subsequent "all-in" execution."
    3. "Testing is a significant, permanent part of our ongoing optimization efforts."
- To what degree is your answer to the question above the right one for your business, and why? Or, if it's not the right one, what barriers keep you from shifting to a different level?
    1. Technology and/or infrastructure barriers
    2. People resource levels and/or experience levels
    3. Senior leadership preferences are inappropriate to what decisions require

9

The Importance—and Limitations—of Storytelling

For in much wisdom is much grief: and he that increaseth knowledge increaseth sorrow.

—Ecclesiastes 1:18[1]

It's almost trite to suggest that any good presentation of analysis needs to tell a story, but of course it's true. We're wired for stories. Our primitive brains evolved to detect patterns so we could perceive anomalies that might mean danger. This didn't just mean distinguishing the tips of a lion's ears from a field of tall brown grass—it also meant story arcs with causes and effects. Our experiences create expectations, and stories have historically been powerful means for how we pass along our knowledge about these expectations. And so, effective storytelling has been carefully studied and refined since classical times (and likely longer). If this seems a bit musty a reference for a modern business book, have a peek at how modern practitioners are applying Aristotle's *ethos*, *pathos*, and *logos* modes of rhetoric.[2]

Translated into the modern business world, where on a daily basis we need not only to communicate, but to *persuade* to action in

---

[1] King James Bible, Cambridge edition.
[2] Kate Verrill, "Ethos, Pathos, Logos," *Gamestorming*, April 5, 2011, http://www. gogamestorm.com/?p=634.

a data-rich (and thus potentially confusing) context, well-told stories are not only guides but also powerful noise filters. And here is the source of tension for today's analyst. You appreciate nuance. You've read Nassim Taleb's *The Black Swan*[3] and Daniel Kahneman's *Thinking, Fast And Slow* (which we discuss in the next chapter). So Taleb's concept of the "narrative fallacy" and Kahneman's cautions about our inherent biases for seeing strong causes where they are weak or nonexistent, are front and center for your thinking. And so, you proceed logically and methodically, up from the data, clearly describing what variation you can and can't explain in your models, always cautioning: "Remember, correlation's not causality."

Your audience, on the other hand, doesn't like nuance. Even in a high-functioning organization, they want you to "boil it down," to give them the "bottom line." (In less well-functioning organizations, they may already have the answers they want in mind, but that's a different problem.) At least in my experience, this will tend to be even more strongly the case in sales organizations. Senior sales executives have alpha personalities that tend to impatience and distractibility inside the walls of the firm, perhaps as a relief from the careful listening and relationship cultivation skills they have had to cultivate to be effective in selling themselves and managing others who do. On the marketing side, many executives will have come from a communications background, and so even if they are more patient about getting to the punch line, their focus may often be on how well the story is told rather than necessarily on its substance. The modern "analytic marketer" is still more the exception than the rule. In any event, getting your message through isn't just about your signal's accuracy but about its strength as well—and packaging is a signal booster.

You have to strike a balance between a core story signal conveying cause and effect to predict outcomes and inform recommendations,

---

[3] Nassim Taleb, *The Black Swan*, (Random House, 2007).

and conveying enough about the noise—the distributions around your "mean" message—that you have responsibly framed the story. Probably the most common way of doing this is to select and assign probabilities to scenarios for different predictions you make based on your analysis, which then support your recommendations (if you're going as far as making them). Gartner, the technology analyst firm, has probably done one of the most memorable jobs of branding its use of scenarios; for example, it explicitly speaks of "$p=0.7$" in describing the dominant scenario in its forecasts.

But don't stop at scenarios. The next step should be to evaluate the stakes associated with a decision. This includes the magnitude of costs and benefits at hand. It also covers the "optionality" associated with pursuing them. Optionality means whether and how you can split up your implementation to gauge whether or not outcomes are tracking predictions. For example, digital advertising via banner ads has much higher optionality than a television ad campaign. The cost of production and media is lower per-unit, so you have the flexibility to test and adjust creative executions, and the ads can be targeted much more closely—than with broadcast television—in terms of who sees them and when. So if the decision at hand is whether to proceed with a television campaign based on predictions about sales it might generate, if the predicted scenarios that would green light the campaign only sum to a 70% likelihood, and your audience can accept no less than 85% certainty, this is worth calling out explicitly. Also, you can use this "stakes-framing" proactively to scope your analysis. By asking decision makers about the necessary burden of proof or confidence level in advance of your work, you can plan schedules and resources more effectively for your investigation.

Summing up, here is one simple outline for an effective sales and marketing analytic presentation that balances the need for a core story with the need for nuance and context:

- "Thank you for your time today..."

- "We're here today because you/we have noticed metric x has declined by y and we need to improve it to z..."

  - (This will be more powerful if it's framed in the context of a broader analytic map, like the one we introduced in Chapter 7, "Practical Analytics—Knowing When to Say When.")

- "This analysis considers the following possible levers and options within the scope of what we could use, in the next n months, to close that performance gap..."

  - (Many presentations are critiqued as sounding academic and forcing the executives consuming the analysis to make this linkage. If you do it for them, you get two benefits: you ease their cognitive workload and you also confirm the object of your analysis. For example, you might ask, before proceeding from this section, "I'd just like to check—does this scope still apply? Are there any changes, drops, or additions we should factor in as we talk today and afterward?")

- "So, here are the questions we would need to answer, and the outcomes we'd have to predict, to decide what to do..."

  - (Leave plenty of room here. Ask, "These seemed to us to balance being focused with being comprehensive—any comments on these, or other things you'd like us to address?")

- "We'll start with a base-case story about who our target customer is and how they behave that is foundational to understanding his/her reaction to options for sales and marketing approaches..."

  - (Here again is where the Venus-oriented customer experience approach is a good place to start. As you talk about how the target customer engages with and is influenced by your marketing and sales touch points, it also introduces the opportunity to a) note places where you may be over- or under-invested, and b) where attribution analysis might suggest

some indirect effects between one channel and another—
"Person X sees TV ad, and searches for us via Google on his
or her iPad while watching the show.")

- "We'll flesh that story out by describing the data underneath
  it, and some information about our general logic and specific
  models based on that data—in particular how much variation
  in those behaviors we can explain..."

  - (Remember here that a picture is worth a thousand words.
    Use graphs aggressively. You might even go so far as to use
    visualization tools like Tableau or Spotfire to bring your data
    to life. These in particular make it easier to illustrate how
    your data is distributed when you dimensionalize it through
    important customer or product attributes.)

- "Then we'll re-frame our basic story as a principal scenario, along
  with a few others that also have meaningful probabilities..."

  - (It's generally best to have a main case (60-70% probabil-
    ity), a better case (15-20%), and a less good case (15-20%) in
    mind, linked explicitly to the few main variables that influ-
    ence them, plus maybe a fourth case (0-10%) that addresses
    what happens if some harder-to-predict variables break one
    way or another.)

- "Finally, we'll examine the stakes and optionality associated
  with our options..."

  - (You might examine the minimum sums and lead time
    requirements of the options you outlined at the start.)

- "With that, we'll come to a recommendation for what we
  think you can do now, and what we think we should examine
  further..."

  - (Bring it home! If you are uncomfortable pushing to a spe-
    cific recommendation, try suggesting some tests. The more
    you can link your work to near-term actions that stem from
    it, the more credible you and your team will be.)

Some discussion questions:

- What's the most effective analytic presentation you've seen recently?
- Let's judge that objectively: What recent presentation generated the swiftest drive to action?
- What made the presentation effective?
- How could it have been improved?
- What's unique to the circumstances of the subject matter, and what can be documented as a best practice, to be repeated in your shop?
- Have you recorded, or can you record (screencast with voice-over, live video), the presentation?

10

Managing Bias—Like Air, Invisible and Everywhere

Wikipedia's "List of cognitive biases" page runs to nearly one hundred ways we either twist or ignore facts we are presented with—and these are just the ones related to decision-making, behavior, and beliefs.[1] However, conventional economic thinking of the past several decades has depended on the assumption that people act rationally in making decisions, relying on fully engaged logical faculties. Many routine presentations of analytic findings seem to be built on this assumption as well.

The psychologist Daniel Kahneman, author of the best-selling book *Thinking, Fast and Slow*, which summarizes much of his research with his collaborator Amos Tversky, has provided a very helpful guide to understanding the mechanisms that underlie our biases and to compensating for them. Kahneman distinguishes between "System 1" thinking, which is our tendency to react quickly and impulsively, with "System 2" thinking, which involves a more deliberate consideration of the matters at hand. In contrast with conventional assumptions, Kahneman's and Tversky's research suggests our processing is dominated by System 1 thinking, especially in people who, for a variety of reasons, have either temporarily impaired (for example,

---

[1] "List of biases in judgment and decision making," http://en.wikipedia.org/wiki/List_of_biases_in_judgment_and_decision_making.

sleep-deprived) or less developed System 2's. This chapter explores certain tendencies that are common in the communication and application of marketing and sales insights, and relates experiences for dealing with them.

What Kahneman and Tversky described as System 1 thinking evolved as a mechanism through which we learned pattern matching to help us identify things that don't fit (potential dangers) in our environment. Speaking of one aspect of how it operates, Kahneman says, "The measure of success for System 1 is the coherence of the story it manages to create."[2] In the context of the subconscious and quick-reacting nature of System 1, one relevant consequence of this feature is a tendency to jump to conclusions. This might be fine when a formal but simple review process (say, one that applies Bayesian analysis[3]) suggests a high confidence that initial indications are correct and the cost to implement based on this belief is low, both in terms of input costs and output consequences. But how do you proceed when uncertainty is greater and the stakes are higher? Kahneman suggests that under those circumstances, the right way to proceed is not necessarily "answer first," with data and a single conclusion. Rather, he suggests, start with analytic requirements for a good decision. You might start with possible options for action you could pursue; next, you would identify things you would have to be satisfied with in order to select one from among them, and finally you would present the data relevant to those things, leaving it to the group to conclude which (if any) of the options make sense.

Kahneman's book is a truly wonderful must-read (several times at first, and then once a year) for anyone communicating or consuming analyses. But it has one flaw: I find it too big to carry around in my head and apply in everyday settings. So I've boiled it down into

---

[2] Kahneman, Daniel, *Thinking, Fast and Slow*, New York: Farrar, Straus and Giroux, 2011. p.85.

[3] "Bayesian inference," http://en.wikipedia.org/wiki/Bayesian_inference.

a simple construct I can remember, which at the very least tries to capture the spirit of his research and conclusions, and I apply this regularly in my own work.

The construct here is presented as if I'm a consumer of the analysis being offered, but of course it can also be applied as a checklist of considerations if I'm the presenter. It has three categories: the first is an assessment of the analysis being presented, and of the conclusions being drawn; the second considers the presenter and the presentation itself; and the third evaluates the state of the listener.

Whenever I'm presented with some analysis, I try to work backward from potential decisions I might have. As noted above, I ask myself what I would have to believe in order to pursue any particular option. Then, before considering the logic and conclusions of the presenter, I like to understand the characteristics of the data on which the analysis is based. How much data is there? Is it sufficiently relevant to the questions we need to answer? (Recall the Big Data conundrum of "the drunk looking for his keys under the lamp post" we discussed in Chapter 1, "Strategic Alignment—First You Need to Agree on What to Ask.") As Scott McDonald suggested, we should ask: How is the data distributed? What trends do we see in it? How was it gathered and processed into what I'm seeing?

In many cases, the analysis presented is based on a sample. So, I ask myself whether the sample is appropriately sized and whether answers are appropriately weighted for any sampling biases we need to consider. Then, I ask myself whether there are any past similar studies (asking similar questions of the same data) I can compare this work to, and what their findings have been, so we can assess whether any differing answers are different enough to represent a signal beyond the noise of prior variations in results. If they are, depending on the stakes involved—the costs and potential benefits of action or inaction—and the time available to act, I might wait and re-sample, to see whether the findings are just one-time outliers that end up regressing to the mean next time around.

While I'm taking in the analysis, I try to be sensitive to the presenter and the presentation. Do I have a prior experience or relationship with this person that could color my intake? Are the materials groomed to a fault? (I try to pay attention to grammar, punctuation, sourcing, labeling, and effective graphics. If the presenter has done these well, I could overestimate the quality of the underlying analysis.) Has the person laid out the questions and issues to be considered (apropos of Einstein's quote earlier in the book) thoughtfully? Is the story being presented too tight to be true? Has the presenter anchored me in any ways that might affect my perception of opportunities for improvement—for example, used a one-time, infrequent (a peak or a low), or unlikely benchmark?

Finally, I try to be mindful of my own state of mind, and, if possible, try to read others'. If I'm tired, my System 2 will be compromised and I'll be more likely to let my System 1 jump to conclusions. We all have tendencies to over-emphasize low probabilities. We value potential losses more highly than potential gains. We are unduly influenced by things we may have heard recently, or that, for whatever reason, may have been more memorable. Some, either through long or recent experience, may be overconfident. We overestimate causality, because it's essential to the stories our System 1's crave. We are influenced by the questions and comments of others.

I keep a copy of the chart in Figure 10.1 pasted on a 3x5 card in my notebook so I can quickly remind myself of some of these considerations. It does not do full justice to the Wikipedia list, or to Kahneman's book, so I occasionally go back to those and redo the chart as needed. But I'm satisfied that even if it's not perfect, it's been useful to me many times.[4] Plus, it makes an excellent "Bias Bingo" game card for diagnosing the extent and direction of biases in management team meetings!

---

[4] Two other extremely useful resources I look to quite often are a sample size calculator http://www.surveysystem.com/sscalc.htm and a Bayesian Inference calculator http://instacalc.com/3173.

Managing Bias Checklist

Analysis	Presenter / Presentation	Me / Audience
• Decision? • Stakes? • Time to act? • Relevant questions? • Relevant data? • Amount of data? • Distribution? • Trend? Noise range? • How gathered? • How processed? • Sample size? • Sampling method? • Consistency vs. similar studies?	• Prior experience / relationship? • Story tightness? • Grooming? • Anchoring?	• Energy? • Distraction? • Recent? • Memorability? • Over-emphasizing low probabilities? • Excessively risk averse? • Over-valuing the present: • Over-confidence? • Over-estimating causality? • Influenced by others? • Confirmation?

Figure 10.1 Managing Bias Checklist

Some discussion questions:

• Take the scorecard to the next three or four meetings you go to. What biases do you observe?

• What's behind them?

• What recent decisions have you made that may have been unduly influenced by some of the biases mentioned here?

• How would your decision have been different if you had been aware and had compensated for the biases you now perceive?

• What adjustments can you and should you make to decisions already taken?

• What structural changes to decision-making can you make to better sense and compensate for biases?

Part III
Making Progress

11

Managing Pace and Results—
Momentum Is Strategic

Well-managed analytical organizations are focused on meaningful business results and understand that time is a currency, too. They manage their efforts as a portfolio of investments the way a venture capitalist would, holding each individual analysis to "gates" that must be successfully transited in order to get further funding for experimentation and operationalization. They administer this portfolio with discipline, adhering to a process that assures consistent quality and tracking mechanisms that assure accountability. They make infrastructure, people, and other investments within an "envelope," bounded by potential value and time, that justifies these investments, rather than as open-ended shopping sprees.

"Time is the fire in which we burn"[1]

Most sales and marketing organizations operate on relatively tight cadences and short cycles. There's an annual cycle, of course, but also quarterly and monthly ones. A retailer in the holiday shopping season will be tracking sales daily and weekly. Some, like HSN, even track and manage down to the minute of airtime.

---

[1] Delmore Schwartz, "Calmly We Walk Through This April's Day," *In Dreams Begin Responsibilities*, (1938).

As we've discussed elsewhere in this book, analytics organizations live and breathe through the actions they inform and the results those actions ultimately achieve. These take place in the context of the cycles described above. So, to a significant degree, analytic efforts need to fit into these cycles as well. In well-run analytic shops, this isn't just a matter of generating reports that match the frequency or intensity of operations; it's about working with the operations teams to interpret and analyze these reports for insights about what to do next. At the same time, analytics groups need to have a different gear they can shift into that supports more foundational, exploratory work beyond the bustle of regular operational cycles.

Also, operating groups need time to absorb insights and their implications. Finally, there are the timescales on which the analytic organization's "investors" judge whether their commitments of resources are paying dividends. In many cases, their perceptions of returns are conditioned by the timescales to which they themselves are held accountable. In most organizations, for executives at that level, these are balanced between quarterly and annual results. Todd Purcell's observations about the pace of marketing efforts at USAA and The Hartford are instructive here.

What does this mean for managing an analytics organization supporting these functions? What overall evaluation cycle should it set for itself, for judging its progress? In our work at Force Five Partners, we've gravitated toward a quarterly review cycle. In each of our client engagements, we join our main client counterparts to present the results of the "portfolio" of work we have been pursuing together with our relevant governing entities—sponsoring executives, senior sales and marketing executive committees, and so on—to review insights, related experiments, and full scale operationalization of successful experiments. This discussion of outputs—what we've learned, and how that has translated to action and in turn driven results—then usefully frames our conversation about inputs, including resource requests as well as "air cover"-type individual or organizational interventions we might need. Melanie Murphy of Bed Bath & Beyond, suggests this cycle is optimal as well.

Within the analytic group, this quarterly cadence forces an iterative, phased approach to analysis (see the "Answer Slam" technique we described in Chapter 7, "Practical Analytics—Knowing When to Say When"), as well as discipline about asking whether the data and insights we have are "good enough" to drive a test, or whether the results of a test justify rolling out more broadly.

Keeping Score

How should you evaluate the effectiveness of an analytics organization? Our experience has been that there are two mechanisms for doing so. One is to hold them accountable for the same metrics that the sales and marketing operational groups are measured by. If a sales executive is tracking sales on a dashboard, her analytic advisor in a sales operations group should be looking at that number side by side with her to try to get underneath the trend and suggest possible options. Another is to articulate a "learning agenda" that encompasses the "high stakes, high uncertainty" issues uncovered through a regular application of the Analytic Brief (or its planning equivalent), and then manage this agenda as a portfolio of investments that are bought and sold on whatever cycle (quarterly, for us) is relevant in your business.

In our business, we've used a metric we call "3-2-1" for this. In each quarter, our objective is to have a certain number of fresh, relevant insights, a certain number of prior insights that are informing live experiments, and a certain number of insights or experiments that are now being scaled to full production. The numbers of each

("3-2-1") are arbitrary but a good starting point for managing expectations. The metric is useful on a number of dimensions. First, it keeps teams focused on answers, as opposed to simply providing reports. Second, it keeps them focused on driving actions from those answers. Third, it helps to make sure a portfolio stays balanced, with a healthy mix across its pipeline. And fourth, with a quarterly cycle overlaid, it keeps efforts short and practical. (If something needs to go beyond a quarter, it can, of course, be phased.)

Investing in Capabilities vs. Harvesting Results

For executives who manage analytics groups, one of the biggest questions is how much time to spend working side by side with analysts to help frame and solve problems and drive results, versus focusing their attention on creating the technical, procedural, and human capabilities that their organizations need to succeed.

When we started Force Five Partners six years ago, we pitched one of our first clients on "helping them to build their marketing analytics capability." The CEO's response was, "That's great, but I'm 20% behind in my direct business. What can you do about that?" For the next several years, this shaped our thinking about how we had to approach our work. Whatever we did, the foundation had to be direct hand-to-hand combat with the issues marketers and salespeople were tackling: "How can we get this holiday shopping campaign to perform better?" "What can we do to make the most of this pharmaceutical product launch, in terms of its impact on key opinion leaders?"

But then we began to notice a pattern. We were consistently stuck in first and second gear. We were able to generate an insight and drive to a limited experiment to prove its worth, but not sustain the re-application of it to inform the evolution of the associated actions consistently. We began to think about why this happened, and it led us to the "eco-systemic conditions" we described in Part I, "Improving Your Odds: Eco-systemic Conditions for Analytic Success." And so we began to think about how we could work both ends to the middle. We moved toward driving investments in foundations—technologies, processes, people, and so on—in phases, with "gates" that demanded, at minimum, live usage in a few short months (as in the case of one marketing automation system we were involved in helping to select and implement) as a way to reduce complexity and mitigate risks. From the other end, we demanded that individual analyses we prioritized had to have potentially repeatable application, as in the case of email effectiveness improvement work we did for another service-sector client. "Two-fers" and "Three-fers" became a standard part of our evaluation lexicon.

We began to think about rules of thumb that could help us to keep these dynamics in balance. A simple one was the notion that we couldn't do the same analysis twice, unless we had somehow evolved our process and tools to make them more effective and efficient, even if in a small way, such as documenting what we had done or re-using metadata that might be applicable across these instances (classifications schemes for email subject lines, for example). Another, as we moved beyond insight toward action, was a metric we ended up calling (in the context of evaluating IT's progress in building what we needed) the "slide to screen ratio" or "ppt versus php."

Simply, it worked like this: You would count the number of components yet to be delivered in an IT architecture chart or slide, and then divide them by the number of components or applications delivered over the same time period looking backward. For example, if the chart said 24 components will be delivered over the next three years, and the same number of comparable items had been delivered over the prior three years, you're running at 1.

Admittedly, the standard's arbitrary and hard to compare across situations. But it's the question that's valuable. In one situation, there's a lot of coding but little sense of where it needs to go, tantamount to trying to drive fast in first gear. In the other, there's lots of ambition, but not much seems to happen—like trying to leave the driveway in fifth gear. When I'm listening to a plan for implementing technology for sales and marketing, I'm not only looking at the slides and the demos, I'm also feeling for the instinct of the authors for balancing insight with action. The best plans always seem to say something like, "Well, here's what we learned—very specifically—from the last 24 months' deployments, and here's what we think we need to do (and not do) in the next 24 months as a result." They're simultaneously thoughtful and action-oriented. Conversely, when I don't see this *specifics*-laden reflection and instead get a generic look forward (and a squishy, over-hedged, non-committal roadmap for getting there), warning bells go off.

Pushing for the implications of the answer—to downshift, or upshift, and how—is incredibly valuable. Above "1," pushing might sound like, "OK, so what pieces of this vision *will you* ship in each of the next four quarters, and what critical assumptions and dependencies are embedded in your answers?" Below "1," the question might be, "So, what complementary capabilities, as well as security, usability, and scalability enhancements, do you anticipate needing to make these innovations commercially viable?" The answers you get in that moment—a *Blink*[2]-style test of the insight/action balance—are more useful than any six-figure IT process or organizational audit will yield.

---

[2] Gladwell, Malcolm, *Blink: The Power of Thinking Without Thinking*, (Little, Brown 2005).

Some questions for discussion:

- What's your core cadence? Is it appropriate to the needs of the business?
- What have you contributed recently to improving key business metrics?
- How are you doing versus "3-2-1"?
- What's your "php-ppt" ratio?
- What should you keep, change, drop, or add as a consequence?

12

Governance Models—Because Analytics Are Political

Reflect once again on Judah Phillips' memorable comment, "If information is power, then analytics are inevitably a political process." Every political process includes considerations like who will control what resources, who will participate, and who will play what role in decisions related to the use of those resources. The resources in question are data, analysts, and the people and tools that act on the insights analysts generate from data. Control of these resources means having the right and the budget to buy and sell data and technology, as well as to hire and fire staff and advisors. The decisions at hand include defining data, governing its access, setting priorities for analytic teams, choosing what insights to test and what test results to operationalize, and so on.

Control of data is a tricky thing. Some data is highly sensitive; leaks in information about the magnitudes, costs, and profitability of customer segments, product lines, or processes could compromise your competitive position. On the other hand, locking-down data limits *ad hoc* exploration by analysts for potential insights and by operators to manage their execution more effectively and accountably. And since data's always in flux and needs to be re-validated continuously, there's a temporal element to the control dilemma: When is it appropriate to release "good enough" data quickly, versus taking more time to make sure it's "right"? There's also a cost dimension: Collecting (or buying) information, then organizing it and making it available, is expensive. If you distribute these costs too aggressively, you inhibit exploration and innovation, whereas if you don't impose any cost on the usage of data, you limit accountability for usage of the resource.

Our executives struck an interesting balance. They favored maximizing analysts' access to data, essentially granting them a "golden ticket" to get what they felt they needed, within logistically feasible parameters (for example, getting a batch job to dump records from a production system is something that needs to be scheduled so it doesn't interfere with day-to-day operations). At the same time, they were inclined to force a discipline on analysts to justify their requests by cobbling together preliminary cuts using samples, trials, free data, and other accessible proxies for the materials they requested. In other words, the consensus from our conversations was that the ticket may be golden, but the check isn't blank.

Control of analysts is even trickier. Where an analytics team lives and whom it reports to inevitably shapes the questions that get asked, and at least the hypotheses for answers, if not the answers themselves. Some of the choices related to *where* include:

- Deciding to position a team at the center, versus distributing it.
- Placing it under the sales or marketing functional heads, versus the leaders of finance or IT, or on its own.
- Managing it as an ongoing "initiative" with a multi-executive steering group, versus institutionalizing its existence.

All of these choices have tradeoffs that must be considered carefully. The axes of these tradeoffs include:

- Analytic objectivity versus operational intimacy (the closer your analysts are to the people and processes that execute on insights, the better equipped they may be to develop and filter for actionable ideas; the flip side of this is of course the risk of "going native," or becoming so close to the *status quo* that you don't challenge it).

- A focus on "supply" of data versus "demand" for insights (critical mass of analytic expertise and associated *esprit* versus an understanding of the business nuances of the relevant operations being supported).

- Power balance versus organizational complexity. (In other words, you can choose to keep reporting lines clean and give one executive control of the analytic function, or you can matrix-report the group, or have multiple groups reporting to different functions with somewhat overlapping responsibilities and live with the potential rivalries that might create.)

The conversations for this book did not suggest a single optimum outcome, but they did suggest a center of gravity. The senior executives with the most direct experience managing analytic groups, and having to live with their consequences, tended to favor centralization, but they also noted that they employ significant hedging mechanisms to keep their groups from being too isolated, including co-location with and rotations through business groups. In general, the executives we spoke with noted that these analytic capabilities are generally best positioned on the "business" side of the house, rather than in finance or IT. And they favored "steering committees" to complement unified management under a single executive, in order to provide a forum for the broader organizational buy-in that their work inevitably requires, whether it's to do with access to data or taking action based on the insights of the group's work.

Some discussion questions:

- How well aligned are "the stars" to get data and resources into your analytics organization(s), and to take actions based on what comes out of your efforts?

- How well aligned are the issues your analytics organization is exploring with the top priorities in the strategic plans published by sales and marketing?

- How frequent and constructive is the feedback your analytic organization gets on the work it's doing?

- How much do you find you have to re-cover ground with various executives to explain the structure and agenda of your analytics organization, versus being able to build on such prior awareness and focus on specific business issues?

- Are other senior executives keeping score the same way you are about your analytic efforts?

13

"Culturelytics"—A Practical Formula for Change

A common denominator in all the conversations for this book is the importance of culture. Culture makes building an analytics capability possible. In some cases, as for Doug Collier at La-Z-Boy, pressure for culture change comes outside-in: external conditions become so dire that a firm must embrace data-driven objectivity. In others, such as for David Norton at Harrah's, the pressure comes top-down: Senior leadership embodies it, leads by example, and is willing to re-staff the firm in its image. But, as for many of the other executives, what do you do when the wolf is not quite at the door, or when it makes more sense (hopefully, your situation) to try to build the capability largely within the team you have than to make wholesale changes?

There are a lot of models for understanding culture and how to change it. Figure 13.1 presents a caveman version (informed by behavioral psychology principles, and small enough to remember). Culture is a collection of values or beliefs, themselves built on count-less observations about what works and what doesn't: what behaviors lead to good outcomes for customers, shareholders, and employees, and what behaviors are either ignored or punished.

$$C = \sum_{V=1}^{n} V$$

Figure 13.1 Culture is the Sum of Values

Values, in turn, are *developed* through chances individuals have to try target behaviors (and observations of others' chances), the consequences of those experiences, and how effectively those chances and their consequences are communicated to other people working in the organization. Figure 13.2 summarizes this relationship.

$V = f(cha, con, com)$

Figure 13.2 Values are a Function of Chances, Consequences, and Communication

Chances are to culture change as reps (repetitions) are to sports. If you want to drive change, to get better, you need more of them. Remember that not all reps come in games. Test programs can support culture change the same way practices work for teams. Also, *courage is a muscle*: to bench press 500 pounds once, start with one pushup, then ten, and so on. If you want your marketing team to get comfortable conceiving and executing bigger and bolder bets, start by carving out, frequently, many small test cells in your programs. Then, add weight: Define and bound dimensions and ranges for experimentation within those cells that don't just have limits, but also minimums for departure from the norm. If you can't agree on exactly what part of your marketing mix needs the most attention, don't study it forever. A few pushups won't hurt, even if it's your belly that needs the attention. A habit is easier to re-focus than it is to start.

Consequences need to be both visible and meaningful. Visible means good feedback loops to understand the outcome of the chance taken. "Meaningful" can run to more pay and promotion of course, but also to opportunity and recognition. And don't forget: A sense of impact and accomplishment can be the most powerful reinforcement of all. For this reason, a high density of chances with short, visible feedback loops becomes really important to your change strategy.

Communication magnifies and sustains the impact of chances taken and their consequences. If you speak up at a sales meeting, the client says, "Good point," and I later praise you for that, the culture change impact is X. If I then relate that story to everyone at the next sales team meeting, the impact is X times 10 others there. If we write down that behavior in the firm's sales training program as a good model to follow, the impact is X times 100 others who will go through that program.

Summing up, here's a simple set of questions to ask for managing culture change:

- What specific values does our culture consist of?
- How strongly held are these values? How well reinforced have they been by chances, consequences, and communication?
- What values do I need to keep, change, drop, or add?
- In light of the pre-existing values "topology"—a fancy way of saying the values already out there and their relative strength— what specific chances, consequences, and communication program will I need to effect the necessary keeps, changes, drops, and adds to the value set?
- How can my marketing and sales programs incorporate a greater number of formal and informal tests? How quickly and frequently can we execute them?
- What dimensions (for example, pricing, visual design, messaging style and content, and so on) and "min-max" ranges on those dimensions should I set?
- How clearly and quickly can we see the results of these tests?
- What pay, promotion, opportunity, and recognition implications can I associate with each test?

- What mechanisms are available and which should I use to communicate tests and results?

Ask these questions daily, tally up the score—chances taken, consequences realized, communications executed—weekly or monthly. Track the trend, and then slice the numbers by the behaviors and people you're trying to influence and the consequences and communications that apply. Don't forget to keep culture change in context; frame it with the business results the culture is supposed to serve. Refocus, then wash, rinse, repeat. Very soon you'll have a clear view of and strong grip on culture change in your organization.

Some discussion questions:

- How analytics-friendly is your current culture?

- Specifically, are there plenty of chances to apply insights, are the consequences favorable to generating insights and experiences, and is there a good communication capability in place to reinforce successes and lessons?

- Name five *ur*-stories about the success or failure of past analytic exploits that have driven the current analytic climate in your firm. What songs are sung of heroes who developed business-changing insights and the glory that followed? What cautionary tales are whispered of wild goose chases that bounced off the management team's atmosphere, taking analysts with them?

- What's similar or different about them? Are their heroes concentrated in any particular way? Is there a recurring focus of their labors? What can you infer from similarities or differences in their plots?

Part IV
Conversations with Practitioners

14

Conversations with Practitioners

Paul Magill

Chief Marketing Officer
Abbott

Paul Magill, a former Monitor Group colleague, is now the Chief Marketing Officer at Abbott. Having advised Abbott as a McKinsey consultant on issues related to the Abbvie spinoff, Paul was recruited to Abbott by CEO Miles White in late 2012. Urbane and good-humored as always, Paul was kind enough to be the first person I interviewed for this book.

After the separation of the proprietary pharmaceuticals business, the remaining Abbott business is a blend of general medicines, diagnostic devices, and nutritional products (such as *Similac* for infants and *Ensure* for adults). With decisions in these categories made as much by the patient as by recommendations from doctors, Abbott is more consumer-focused in its outreach. As such, Abbott now counts firms such as Johnson & Johnson and Nestlé as competitors more so than traditional pharmaceutical firms.

Abbott is a global business and has historically been managed in a very decentralized way through a product- and region- based structure. This degree of delegation and discretion fostered a highly accountable culture, but also a proliferation of processes and infrastructure and a natural aversion to "help from corporate." The firm's 12 businesses, organized in four groups, have performed well in business terms but have been somewhat less governed from a brand perspective, each communicating more or less in ways it sees fit for its remit. This, in turn, has resulted in a relative under-projection of the firm's reputation among certain audiences, including investors.

Abbott's opportunities also run beyond brand integration. Abbott's nutritional businesses have been very successful, but it's important that the firm accelerates growth in its other segments. In support of this, in his role as CMO, Paul has described two missions. One is to drive the corporate identity—to balance the Abbott brand architecture across its product, division, and corporate components. This is crucial because consumers of the individual product lines are not the only audiences to be influenced. There are also pharmacists, Key Opinion Leaders, governments, and prospective employees, in addition to investors. The other is to enhance Abbott's marketing capabilities overall—to make sure that each group is maximizing its potential, and to see that best practices are appropriately shared across the groups.

In support of these objectives, Paul recently created a Global Marketing Council. Crucially, this group has clout; its membership includes the division CEOs. Together, these members are creating "The Abbott Way" of marketing. Paul has introduced the "Abby Kohnstamm IBM model" as one approach. (Abby was brought in by Lou Gerstner as IBM's SVP of Marketing in 1993, introduced an integrated marketing approach to the firm, and consolidated agency relationships into a global arrangement with Ogilvy & Mather; many readers may remember the "Solutions for a Small Planet" campaign—including nuns touting the firm's technologies[1]—an iconic campaign that helped to clarify, update, and amplify the firm's message at a crucial time in the industry.) Ordinarily driving necessary consensus at this level, among leaders of businesses with very different contexts and objectives can be certainly a tough management challenge, but Paul has his CEO's support for what he's trying to do.

---

[1] "Solutions for a Small Planet," IBM, 1994, http://youtu.be/HmQ3f1PRnw0.

Another dimension of the challenge is the need to bring Abbott's digital marketing capabilities to the front. Paul inherited a highly varied collection of websites and underlying tech stacks, less suited to run rich media, with no single content management system, and no digital asset management system. But in addition to his experience as a marketer, Paul has a well-developed knowledge of technology, which he gained during his time at IBM. This has made it straightforward for him to partner with Abbott's CIO for the technical transformation that inevitably must accompany the strategic one. To accelerate progress, more recently Abbott has been working with Sapient to update and rationalize the firm's digital marketing footprint.

With this rationalization will come—is now coming—an *analytic* transformation for Abbott's marketing function as well. Paul has created a new, centralized marketing intelligence function, in part because he needs to make sure he balances the typical cultural preference for applying analytics to demand and lead generation marketing with attention to the brand marketing mission he's trying to support. This is especially important given that he expects the refreshed brand to be digitally- and socially-centric in both experience and in media investment. Paul says he's particularly influenced by frameworks that help to understand the buying process, such as the "Channel Pathways" framework developed at Monitor Group (in its Marketspace unit, and referred to in Chapter 5, "Practical Frameworks—For Getting On the Same Page"), and more recently the "Customer Decision Journey" articulated by McKinsey's David Edelman.

But sequencing matters here especially. To get value from analytic insights, Paul's assessment has been that he needs, at this stage, to focus as much or more on prescribing a shared model for marketing capability development as on "results-back" management by marketing objectives. To reinforce this, and to complement the consensus he's driving through the Global Marketing Council, he's created regional marketing teams that report to him but that work in the field with the general managers of different business units. In parallel, he's in the process of beefing up the firm's digital and social marketing capabilities. Coordinating all this change across the globe (when we spoke, Paul had recently returned from Vietnam) makes it an even more daunting proposition, but it's an exciting challenge as well!

Doug Collier

Chief Marketing Officer & President, International
La-Z-Boy Incorporated

Doug Collier is the Chief Marketing Officer of La-Z-Boy Incorporated, makers of the iconic recliner we all know, but also of a broad spectrum of high-quality, contemporary furniture. I was introduced to Doug by Joe Fuller, one of the founding partners of the international strategy consulting firm Monitor Group, who now teaches at Harvard Business School. Joe has been working with HBS Professor Michael Porter to research American competitiveness, and La-Z-Boy's dramatic comeback story is the focus of one of Joe's case studies.

Furniture is mostly a discretionary purchase, and the effects of the 2008 crash on the housing industry were especially acute for furniture makers—especially for higher-end firms. However, under Chairman and CEO Kurt Darrow's leadership, La-Z-Boy adapted aggressively to changing conditions. The firm not only closed a number of plants to reduce costs, but also fortunately, just prior to the downturn, had changed the way it approached manufacturing, evolving toward much more flexible and efficient cellular techniques that allowed it to better meet what demand did exist.

The urgency to change (at the time of the crisis, La-Z-Boy had to find a way to cut its cost structure dramatically in 90 days—up to 20–25% of costs in some areas) brought a heightened focus on efficiency, innovation, and accountability on the manufacturing side of the business, and more specifically the increased and expanded utilization of lean management approaches and tools such as 6-Sigma, Kaizen, and 5S, all with common denominators of objectivity through data, root-cause orientation, and reliance on hypotheses and testing as means for driving and acting on insight. Inevitably, these began to spread beyond manufacturing. As Doug puts it, "Manufacturing upped its game, and so we in marketing needed to as well."

It also needed to retake control of its retail channel—and with this, to learn to be an effective retailer as well as a manufacturer. (To speed this, the firm brought on Mark Bacon, a veteran senior executive with past roles at Pep Boys, Walmart, and Staples—all firms with reputations for disciplined, data-driven management.)

Under Doug's stewardship, the marketing organization at La-Z-Boy has also undergone a significant transformation. La-Z-Boy was known for its iconic recliners, but had a much broader offering and needed to realize the growth potential within its addressable markets. It also needed to reach women more effectively in order to do that, since they represent a disproportionate share of furniture shoppers.

Doug describes three pie charts that became foundational communication pieces for its growth plans. The first notes that, among folks shopping for recliners, a quarter will visit La-Z-Boy stores. The second notes though that when folks are shopping for a recliner *and* some other piece of furniture, that figure drops to 19%. Finally, the third notes that among shoppers looking for only stationary furniture, only 4% would look inside a La-Z-Boy store. Doug says, "There was little doubt about the size of the prize; the question was, could we do it?"

Realizing this potential has come through some big bets and a blend of disciplined testing, both closely monitored through a broader commitment to data-driven marketing. Even as it cut costs by as much as 25% in the dark days of a few years ago, the firm did not appreciably cut its marketing budget. Instead, it chose to invest through the downturn and even to raise the bet by bringing on Brooke Shields as a brand ambassador and committing to an advertising campaign with a national scope. Says Doug, "Signing Brooke wasn't something you could do as a test. We had to go, but we felt combining Brooke's appeal with our prior brand equity would lead our target customers to give us a chance. On the other hand, we didn't just jump; we did a lot of careful qualitative and quantitative research on our brand platform to shape our advertising. We didn't want to make Brooke the brand, but rather have her be the vehicle through which our target customers could discover that our product line fits their lifestyle, and that our stores are great places to shop." The firm has done seventeen spots with Brooke so far, and has the analytic infrastructure in place (including the use of extensive quantitative and qualitative testing of the spots in primary research, and the YouGov *BrandIndex* service extended with some custom questions focused on the awareness and effect of the brand platform) to understand, scientifically, which spots, in what combinations, are effectively conveying which messages at different times.

The firm has been equally aggressive on the digital front. Doug noted he's been fortunate to have a very strong head of interactive, Matt Targett, who came to La-Z-Boy from Classmates.com. Matt acted very early to integrate social (Pinterest, for example) and mobile channels into La-Z-Boy's digital experience. Also, Doug has a uniquely strong relationship with IT: The CIO reports to him! This structure has facilitated both the sourcing and the use of data to drive the evolution of the firm's digital presence, as well as extensive collaboration on the development of a web and e-commerce infrastructure that will not only provide great consumer experience but also provide richer analytic opportunities.

Doug noted the importance of an analytically inclined culture as foundational. "It's almost a joke," he says, offering an example of the conversations there, "'If you don't bring me a control group, don't bother talking to me!'" He explained the firm's insistence on a "double-delta": "Don't just tell me how we compare with past performance; I also need to understand the lift over control." So now, "Even the PR and brand guys will come in with numbers to support their suggestions." This base has made it possible for the firm to engage effectively with partners like QualPro and APT (multivariate test programs) and MarketShare Partners (media mix models and simulations).

Notwithstanding, the firm still has challenges absorbing and acting on analytic insights. Doug offers an example, a test of an in-store free gift promotional event, targeted primarily to existing customers, but also selectively to some prospects. The test generated a 90–100% lift in sales. "But of course, once successes like this are identified, they are baselined into your next year's budget," says Doug. However, the firm manages its overall P&L so that it only spends 8–8.5% of sales on promotions of this kind. "So that means that when we're adding new programs, we have to cull old ones, and that can be hard organizationally."

To help push past that challenge, the firm is investing aggressively in attribution analysis. Working with MarketShare Partners, Doug and his team have created a baseline multi-channel attribution model working off three years of historical data. They've cast a wide net for the model, including traditional above-the-line advertising expenditures, as well as digital spending and even to promotional spending by dealers. The model is updated quarterly with fresh data, and Market-Share Partners have built a simulation capability to allow Doug's team to run "What-if?" scenarios. At the moment, re-planning based on suggestions from the model is still done on an annual basis (because of the long cycles for lining up changes to many of the channels considered), but of course Doug hopes to shorten media buying cycles to give the firm more flexibility to adapt to changing conditions, their attendant challenges and opportunities for La-Z-Boy.

But Doug hasn't assumed that "If we build it, they will come." Rather, he's got a broad set of interests represented in the governance of the attribution model and the work by MarketShare. He's found that this group is "very interested in what's under the hood," and he frequently hears, "This doesn't make sense," in reviews of assumptions and outputs from the model, a good sign of engagement and commitment to its continuous improvement. While Doug feels this transparency has contributed positively to organizational absorption, he admits that the objective of making shifts in funds across channels more fluid is still a work in progress—particularly where such shifts go beyond channels he can control to ones where a more influence-oriented approach is necessary. In one case, as he works with dealers, he needs to reconcile differences in their advertising models (for example, a much greater reliance on circulars) with the approaches taken for company-owned stores.

Nonetheless, the investment has paid off so far. In addition to a fairly common discovery that there's room to shift more dollars to digital channels (for example, paid search and display advertising), he's also found more surprising opportunities, such as greater potential leverage from terrestrial and satellite radio. Conversely, he's found that direct marketing was less powerful than he and his team thought going in.

In the course of parsing through these findings and looking for other benchmarks to compare them against, Doug came across *How Brands Grow: What Marketers Don't Know*, by Professor Byron Sharp of The University of South Australia. Professor Sharp argues, and presents supporting evidence, that marketers have swung the pendulum too far to direct marketing/loyalty-oriented/CRM-focused tactics and channels targeted on the "best" 20% of their customers. Reach, he argues, is undervalued today, as is driving trial, even for firms generally playing within established markets and seeking to extend them, rather than growing into new markets where we would expect to see these objectives emphasized more.

Of course, La-Z-Boy's attribution model doesn't stop at broad aggregate conclusions. Doug is working on exploring geographic variances, which in this business one would expect to matter a great deal.

Another factor working in Doug's favor has been a strong relationship with La-Z-Boy's agency of record, RPA (Santa Monica, California). RPA's brief extends across traditional channels and even through digital advertising and SEO. Doug also notes productive experiences with media partners, such as Novus, which the firm relies on to place newspaper ads for company-owned stores in different markets.

To this point, however, one limiter in the productivity of La-Z-Boy's web management has been their web site infrastructure, which today still takes an outside agency's developers to modify. Doug described a new infrastructure program currently underway that will port la-z-boy.com to a new Oracle-Endeca-ATG stack, putting more control of look and feel into the hands of his internal team.

Another limiter is that to date, given resource constraints, the firm hasn't been able to invest in a cross-channel marketing automation platform. Rather, it has outsourced operations channel by channel—for example, using Listrak for direct marketing, and then bringing on a CRM firm and giving them access to the customer database so they can optimize campaigns.

In fact, more generally, given the lie of the marketing ball for the firm, Doug sees bringing more marketing operations inside the firm as a priority ahead of bringing analytics (for example, the work MarketShare Partners is doing) inside. He says, "I believe you have to get more hands-on in using the data, understanding the nuances of the operations, before you can really pursue efficiencies, or you won't understand them as well."

Nonetheless, he is planning to further beef up his in-house analytic resources. He's trading off "creativity" for "analytic rigor, detail-orientation, and specific marketing analytics experience" as he evaluates marketers as candidates for roles on his team. Given the common challenges of recruiting to smaller towns and cities (La-Z-Boy is based in Monroe, Michigan, halfway between Detroit and Toledo on the western shore of Lake Erie), he's opened up his recruiting aperture to consider, for example, financial analysts with demonstrated interests in the marketing discipline. "Really in the end," he says, "it's so much more important to focus on the whole person and get a great one, than to be strict about the specific requirements."

All this work has led to impressive results. Today, 30% of women surveyed are aware of La-Z-Boy's connection with Brooke Shields and the firm's new brand platform. Further, Doug notes that the brand platform, combined with updated merchandising and a new store concept, has contributed to 13 straight quarters of same-store sales growth for the La-Z-Boy store system (averaging double-digits), and a rate of growth of non-reclining product twice the rate of growth of the recliner category.

Scott McDonald

Senior Vice President, Research
Condé Nast Publications

Scott heads market research at Condé Nast, publisher of such iconic titles as *Vogue, The New Yorker, Vanity Fair*, and *Glamour*. I talked with him as he was winding down teaching his fall term course in Columbia's MBA program, "Measuring and Monetizing Media Audiences." Despite a flight back from London spent grading papers, he was his usual gracious self. Scott, who came to the world of media and advertising with a Ph.D. in Sociology from Harvard, laughed wryly at the mention of "Analytics" and its fellow-traveler "new-fangled" terms, noting that he'd never imagined that his training as a statistician and demographer—truly well within the "province of specialists"—would become as "cool" and "hot" as it now seems, for the moment anyway.

Industry Basics

So here's how the magazine business works in the 21st century. Take *Glamour*. There's the advertising side of course, which in *Glamour*'s case contributes approximately 80% (I'm guessing—Condé Nast is privately held) of the title's total revenue. Scott's organization's responsibilities cover advice to both the advertising side of the house as well as sales to readers, which accounts for the balance.

Glamour's print circulation is roughly 2.3 million copies per month.[2] About 300,000 of those are single copies sold at the newsstand, at full price. (Solving for, or at least stemming, the steep decline in newsstand sales is a major priority across the industry.) The rest are sold to subscribers. Initial offers to subscribers are almost always at

---

[2] Neal Lulofs, "The Top 25 U.S Magazines for June 2013," The Alliance for Audited Media, August 6, 2013, http://www.auditedmedia.com/news/blog/2013/august/the-top-25-us-consumer-magazines-for-june-2013.aspx.

deeply discounted promotional prices to get folks to sample, so it's critical to convey these offers as efficiently (and leave as little money on the table with each offer) as possible. Then there are renewals. For publishers, nirvana is getting a subscriber to opt-in for auto-renewal at the full subscription price (a little under $2 per copy for *The New Yorker*—a bargain, to this faithful subscriber) and leave a credit card number on file so no bills and checks need cross in the mail; also, there's less chance your renewing subscribers will take advantage of the next promotional offer. Still rapture, if not quite the perfection of the previous arrangement, is to provide a valid email address with the initial subscription; this can make renewal solicitations more efficient for Condé Nast and more convenient to act on (or ignore) for the subscriber.

Of course, the product itself is getting more sophisticated, for both subscribers and advertisers. Time Inc. is viewed as a leader in this regard; it publishes targeted editions of some of its titles and manages an elaborate house list with many different "sub-files." Further, it's aggressive about renting access to its lists to advertisers, in addition to providing them with tighter addressability—via the targeted editions it prints.

Enter digital. Some publications—*The Wall Street Journal* or *The New York Times*, for example—give you the choice of subscribing to digital-only, print-only, both, or derivatives thereof (some sections, not others, for example, in the case of the *Times*). Others—like my favorite, *The New Yorker*—offer a one-price-for-all model, where digital access and additional products come with the annual subscription to the print version. Now you may ask, "How can they afford to do this?" The answer is that, in addition to providing advertisers with additional access to the subscriber's eyeballs, digital editions and other related digital properties offer a vehicle not only for presenting subscription and renewal offers, but also for gathering data that will make pricing and presenting those offers smarter—in theory, at least.

How Scott Looks at the World

As Scott puts it, "I came up as a statistically-trained sociologist, baptized in the Church Of The Random Sample and educated in The School Of The Normal Distribution. I'd used this training in writing my dissertation, on the nature of processes driving turnover in the real estate markets of Boston's South End." On arriving at Time Inc. as Director of Consumer Research after getting his doctorate, Scott immediately saw some parallels between his training and modeling responses to subscription offers, but also important differences he feels are overlooked in how marketing analysts apply statistics to their work.

Specifically, he notes that the base case taught in academic statistics settings—random (unbiased) samples producing bell-curve distributions—is less common in the world of sales and marketing. This is hardly an esoteric observation. For example, at its most basic, the meaning of an average in a skewed distribution is very different. Take a popular, if problematic, measure of "engagement" used in the media world: average time on page. If 100 people visit your web page, and 97 of them spend one second on it while the other three spend three minutes each on it, your average time on page is over six seconds per visitor, implying, on average, a solid scan at least of the page by the "average" visitor. The problem, Scott observes, is that many analysts today that grapple with big data sets start, rather blindly, with summary statistics about data sets that implicitly assume the academic base case, rather than the marketing and sales realities of biased samples and skewed distributions. Scott pointed to Nate Silver's analysis of recent elections as a good example of the "arbitrage" these assumptions offer: By studying and handicapping the sampling biases of various polls, Silver was able to call each election right down to the very electoral vote count.

Scott suggests that the key is "to begin by asking, 'What distribution do we have in the data?'" To this end, he'll typically start with simple plots: a univariate distribution of a dependent variable to be examined, then maybe bivariate plots of each major potential driver against the object of study. If you understand the distributions of customer characteristics and behaviors well, it's possible to do what he characterizes as "forensic" analysis—examining changes in these distributions. For example, you might notice early, weak signals that a magazine's file (its list of subscribers) may be aging, as the title becomes less appealing to young readers leading the migration to digital frontiers. He likens looking at the evolution of a subscriber file distribution along its multiple dimensions over time to "examining tree rings."

Also, in a world where it's more and more tempting to let machines tell you what's going on in the data, Scott still believes in following a hypothesis-driven approach as "cake," and letting the "emergent" (machine-driven story development) play the role of "frosting". He observes that while this may seem "old school" to some, he finds that hypotheses make it much easier to engage his internal clients in helping to explore potential variables to include in his analysis, to keep an eye out for sampling variations to adjust for as he goes, and ultimately to partner with his clients to judge the truth or falsity of the initial hypothesis to frame a business response. To guard against creeping biases in his own hypothesis development process, Scott tries to be "omnivorous" about data sources that allow him to examine the potential explanatory impact of different customer dimensions (demographic or behavioral).

How Things Work in Practice

Scott notes that the processes magazine publishers use for database marketing haven't really changed since the 1980s: "It's still Direct Marketing 101," he says. File sizes are, in the context of today's Big Data numbers, still very limited—roughly 20 million names in his case. (While subscriber databases are still maintained by the firm, fulfillment is still handled by a third party. So there's always a reconciliation exercise to be done.)

Here are the basics. Let's say you have a list with name and address for each subscriber. You might also append some third party data you can match to the core name and address data, from a vendor like Acxiom or Experian. With this enriched file, you might do some statistical analysis—a straight linear regression, typically—to see what variables describing customers best predict which ones will subscribe at different offer prices. What you're after is trying to establish who, among the population, will take the highest offer, before you start getting more aggressive from there. This assessment is of course probabilistic, not deterministic. So you score each person's propensity, assign him or her to deciles, and then match an affordable/efficient promotional mix to each decile. You're testing these promotional mixes (copy, art, channel, and so on) of course, on top of that. "But," he says, "it's still not Big Data—it's a SQL database, with columns and rows...And besides, data sets are ghastly and inconsistent in many cases"—a problem that size only compounds.

Now, again, enter digital. Condé Nast's digital properties generate lots of data, of course. But, it turns out that there's not a lot of overlap between print readers and digital readers. Most online visitors are coming in from search or from social media. And recall surveys—asking print subscribers what if any part of their online experience motivated them to subscribe or not—are "Basically useless when it comes to digital experiences," says Scott.

However, when visitors come to Condé Nast's digital properties, their servers drop a cookie in the visitor's browser (more on this in a moment). Condé Nast knows where the visitor was referred from, where he or she clicks through to when done, and the full clickstream across Condé-owned sites. Groups of cookies defined by similar clickstream patterns (or cookie pools) can be further enriched by matching Condé Nast cookies with cookies dropped by third party data vendors, who through other means (Acxiom's "Audience Operating System" is a recent example) can begin to paint a clearer picture of the people the cookies represent, though of course not to the level of personally identifiable information (PII), to protect privacy.

Condé Nast has its own method for further enriching data to add proprietary value, called the Preferred Subscriber Network Survey. "It's a doozy of a survey, like MRI's," says Scott. "We reach out to the 20 million people on our list and get 500,000 responses. We then do a 'look-alike' cross with our enriched cookie pool—we call that 'imputation.'" With that, based on a new capability developed by Condé Nast's head of analytics, Chris Reynolds (formerly of Kraft, Digitas, and DoubleClick) and his team, the firm can sell well-founded behaviorally- and demographically-defined segments across all its digital properties to its advertisers and participate in programmatic buying facilitated by third parties (including real time bidding [RTB] for Condé cookies). Scott can also predict the offline behavior (including subscription-related behavior) of his online visitors—allowing him to better target subscription offers to those online visitors.

Complications and Frontiers

Condé Nast's digital editions are increasingly consumed on tablets and smartphones, versus PCs (laptops or desktops). On these form factors, these digital editions, or apps, have software that fire Adobe tracking tags. In theory, this should give us wonderful transparency into how people are interacting. But in practice, there are problems with the data. Apps move you away from the page-based analytics model and toward an event-oriented one, and there are transition and consistency costs associated with this. Also, there's a latency challenge: These form factors may not always be connected to the web.

In any event, Scott does see in the numbers that the consumer's experience is enhanced by the multi-platform delivery Condé Nast can now provide. Renewal rates are up, at higher prices. Multi-platform *New Yorker* readers are re-upping at double the rate of print-only subscribers, for example (though this lift is lower at other titles).

Also, as noted before, most reading is still happening in print—and "It's getting tucked into smaller and smaller crannies, like the short window in airline flights between when the door closes and when it's OK again to turn on your digital devices—though even this is going away too!" says Scott. [*Author's note: Look on the bright side—with Wi-Fi and cell access spreading on planes, the latency problem will decline.*]

While Scott would really love a 360-degree view, he still can't reliably track an individual user across form factors, to relate interaction patterns to subscription behavior. "I get one app ID from the smartphone and another from the tablet," he says. Also, "I'd love to track (anonymously, of course) by integrating with the subscriber file, but Adobe's data doesn't support that yet." And of course he can't really practically track reading in print. What he can do is look at digital-only subscribers, and see whether binge-reading, for example, or registering two versus only one device, are associated with taking renewals at higher rates and prices. And also, analytics on content, independent of association with particular groups of readers, is providing valuable feedback to editors as well.

But Scott suggests that complaints about the precision limitations these issues imply for targeting miss a broader opportunity. If you think strictly like a statistical analyst, you might not be comfortable, given these data problems, with drawing conclusions about who will respond to what necessary to drive a marketing campaign. But if you think a bit more across disciplines, making Nate-Silver-style Bayesian inferences (my simplified definition: "If it walks and quacks like a duck, based on the prior probability of creatures that walk and quack like ducks actually being ducks, chances are good it's a duck..."), you can get comfortable enough to test, and then let the test results round out your thinking for the broader campaign.

Melanie Murphy

Senior Director of Customer & Business Analytics
Bed Bath & Beyond

Melanie Murphy is Senior Director of Customer & Business Analytics at Bed Bath & Beyond. Erica Seidel, an executive recruiter who formerly ran Forrester's CMO Council, introduced me to Melanie. Melanie came to BB&B from Mindtree, an analytic consulting firm and information technology solutions integrator. Earlier in her career, Melanie spent nearly eleven years at Experian, where she led a team of over twenty statisticians and was responsible for all client-facing analytical services delivery. Melanie has a Master's degree in statistics, an achievement she described as a "stall tactic." (We should all procrastinate so productively!) Since that wasn't enough, she also studied operations research, "because I liked math," as she modestly puts it.

A large part of our conversation focused on how to increase the impact an analytics team has on an organization. This included how to shift the analytics team from being reactive "order takers" toward leading the thinking of the organization's decision makers by aligning the team's initiatives to the strategic initiatives of the organization. Melanie strongly believes that "analytics is strategic" and that there are multiple analytic tactics that will directly impact most of an organization's strategic business objectives. Aligning them allows her team to focus their analytic efforts in the areas that will have the highest impact.

Paradoxically—in the sense that you'd expect that objective to drive an analytics team to think ahead of what the organization is currently doing—Melanie feels that a big piece of this is "focusing" analytics to the envelope of what's possible to execute. "If you can't act on a model, for example, you probably shouldn't build it," she says. Considering (in advance) the actions that will be taken from an analysis or how a model will be deployed, directly impacts the way the analysis is conducted or how a model is developed. This type of planning leads to a higher success rate, saves valuable time in rebuilding models, and avoids other "bridge-to-nowhere" analyses.

One important path to increasing an analytics team's impact is to manufacture "at-bats." Melanie believes that it is the responsibility of the analytics leadership team to appropriately pace analytic efforts and measure their success partly as a function of that pace, and to articulate not just the insights found but also the collective performance of the group to the executive team. Melanie finds that monthly and/or quarterly business review meetings are a great venue for this. In addition to addressing matters at hand, Melanie uses these opportunities to "remind them of what we've done and educate them about what we're capable of."

One technique Melanie has used to make sure her team's work stays grounded is to articulate "personas" and "use cases." "This may seem so elementary," she says, "but even though we do a good job of running the company by the usual metrics, we're still working on getting a clearer read of who our customers are...this seems to be a perpetually recurring problem in the industry, based on my experiences stretching back to my days at Experian. As more and more data becomes available, the more there is to learn and relearn about who our customers are and how they want to engage." This sense of identity, personality, and narrative is especially important for implementing and instrumenting "omni-channel" experiences. Without these, she says, "You tend to engineer platforms for any possible interaction, and efforts like those tend to collapse under their own weight." More specifically, Melanie describes several experiences with "leveraging more dimensions of data that didn't lead to more understanding," principally because these efforts were ungrounded in a hypothesis with some reasonable probability.

Melanie is a big believer in the "Center of Excellence" model for organizing analytics capabilities. In her experience, this model works best when it's organized on the "business side" of the house, rather than in IT, and reports up to the head of marketing. For her, the scope of such a group should be broad and responsible for financial reporting for marketing, tracking results for specific campaigns, web analytics, quantitative (including statistical) analysis, research and development, a BI group to support *ad hoc* reporting, and also a group of IT professionals for "data management." (The data management team has responsibility for working with IT to align data definitions, in addition to streamlining capabilities for data access and usage.) Her experience has been that this division of labor is a "really good model."

On the talent front, Melanie noted that a typical pattern she's seen is revealed in how analytic positions are budgeted and staffed. When an analytics team is positioned *reactively,* these open up very quickly in response to some flash of demand and then are retracted equally as quickly as "overhead" when a particular set of questions fade from view or a business opportunity (a new product category, for example) passes from the priority list. This evanescent approach to investing in staffing an analytics team can make it really hard to be appropriately selective, and it's one of the reasons why it's so crucial to *lead* thinking rather than respond to it.

The talent challenge, she notes, has two dimensions. One the one hand, you need subject matter experts. "I can't afford to teach an analyst statistics from the ground up at this point," she observes. But on the other, the specialization of the roles, and the typical analytic personality that tends to fall in love with the analysis itself rather than its application, make orchestrating a team and maximizing its communication capabilities and consequent influence a challenge. Melanie explains, "That's why I don't read analytics books; I try to read books focused on leadership!" One title she's found useful is Tom Davenport's *Competing On Analytics*, especially for the way it's positioned the capability she manages as a differentiating asset senior executives should cultivate, rather than the cost center it's traditionally perceived to be. She also follows the *Harvard Business Review* closely.

Melanie related that it's been easier to find hard-core analytics people than it has been to find good communicators of analytics—people who can break something complex down to manageable pieces and tell a story out of them. She notes that she's had good experience hiring people with backgrounds in economics, as opposed to pure computer science or math backgrounds. More generally, she's found that people who have come into the analytics field from other disciplines where they've had to apply data wrangling and statistical analysis to some other end, tend to do better than people for whom the study of those techniques has been the end rather than the means. Also, she has had great experiences working with people who have taught these subjects before. In fact, one of her favorite interview questions for a quantitative analytics position is, "How would you describe a regression model to a non-mathematician?" For this, as for other questions, she's looking for the thirty-second answer rather than the twenty-minute one. Also, it makes an effective question for a phone screen! At the margin, she says, "I like to find folks who know what I don't, and have done things I haven't. But the core common denominator is, 'Do I think this person will be a good fit culturally? Does he or she value impact as much as insight, and relationships as much as answers?'"

As experienced analysts know, 80% of any statistical analysis is preliminary work to obtain, clean, shape, and explore data. Melanie distinguished between two types of statistical analysts. One group is given their data (in a flat file format) and can do all of their data manipulation and preparation in their statistical tool of choice (like SAS). The other has to go get data. She notes than when she worked for service providers (Experian and Mindtree), in general she was given data that had already been pre-vetted, but it's more typical *not* to have data warehouses that are well–developed, and to have to go get what you need on your own. "Therefore, as you recruit for your team, it is important to understand which group they fall into and how they get to their data," she says. "Otherwise you will end up having to team up a data specialist with a statistical analyst, and this works fine—but only if you can afford it."

Focusing on team dynamics means being able to abstract away, to a certain degree, the successful completion of the work itself. To this end, Melanie has defined a disciplined process for analytic projects based on the hundreds of such efforts she's conducted and led across her career. The process has twelve phases, each with its own process or decision tree, and related resources. Melanie has incorporated her process into a variety of project management tools in different settings, to turn it into a dynamic management tool for her and her teams in those situations. "Applying it consistently has really helped me to review and reflect on what we're doing, not just on getting it done," she says.

With respect to tracking her sector for benchmarks and other analytic perspectives, Melanie finds *MultiChannel Merchant*, and *Marketingcharts.com* to be useful resources. *[Author's note: While at Mindtree, Melanie herself recently authored a very helpful whitepaper titled, "The Five Pillars of Building an Analytics Business Case," that I found very aligned with my own thinking about eco-systemic conditions for analytic success, and useful to improving and extending those ideas.]*

David Norton

Executive Vice President, Customer Analytics & Insights,
MDC Partners
Former Chief Marketing Officer, Harrah's

In a former life, David Norton, currently EVP at MDC Partners, was CMO at Harrah's and Caesars Entertainment. He did his job well enough to be named CMO Of The Year in 2010 by *CMO* Magazine. Notwithstanding more recent challenges from a weak economy, Harrah's (renamed Caesars Entertainment in 2010) has been one of the poster children of the Marketing Analytics Age, featured in such bell-cow titles as Tom Davenport's *Competing On Analytics.* Erica Seidel, who formerly ran Forrester's CMO Council, introduced me to David, and David was kind enough to share some stories and lessons from his experiences.

David started his career at loyalty marketing pioneers MBNA and American Express. He joined Harrah's in 1998, when Harvard Business School Professor Gary Loveman was named COO. As head of relationship marketing initially, David helped to create Harrah's Total Rewards program, which re-thought the traditional practices of lavish coddling on high rollers and emphasized cost-effective cultivation of "average" (frequent-visiting, non-VIPs) patrons by providing them with aspirational tier hurdles.

Culture

One of the first things you need to know about this story is that Gary Loveman (now Caesars' CEO), is a former economist with the Federal Reserve, whose work sought to understand the impact of budget deficits through sophisticated statistical analysis. As David put it, "When your CEO has a Ph.D. from MIT, it kind of sets the tone for the direction of the firm and helps the analysts there feel valued."

This top-down vision led to highly objective, data-oriented capabilities they wanted to build. In particular, Gary's background and

David's experiences and inclinations enabled them to exercise a cultural discipline for fact-based insights. Their reputations helped the firm attract an analytically inquisitive group (including many folks from Wall Street and from strategy consulting firms like Bain and McKinsey) that increased the sophistication of the company's marketing in a collaborative way with its individual properties. Further, as a general rule, he had a preference for "Carnegie Mellon" types with stronger math-oriented backgrounds, as opposed to generalists (even ones with Ivy League backgrounds). Another factor that accelerated the progress he could make in shaping the marketing organization this way was a decision to move the firm's headquarters from Memphis to Las Vegas in 1999. "The leader of our statisticians was a brilliant guy from the University of Nevada at Reno, who really was as much a strategic analytic marketer as he was a statistician. He really understood the marketing realities behind the numbers," says David. "We built the best marketing team in the business," he says, with justified pride.

Relationship with Field Marketing

The next thing to know about this story was that when David started in the business, much of marketing decision-making was decentralized. The firm has properties all over the country, besides, of course, Las Vegas and Atlantic City, and the managers of those properties controlled most of the money for advertising and promotions for their locations. Each one determined its own marketing calendar, around events it wished to promote to drive its profitability. This meant that for David and his team to be effective, rather than resist or ignore that reality, they had to make a fairly intensive consulting model work. Over time this was formalized so that "marketing analysis managers"[3] were embedded in different locations. "One of the best investments we ever made," he says. Another one of the first

---

[3] Koploy, Michael, "David Norton's Four Secrets to Understanding Customers Through Analytics," *Plotting Success*, http://plotting-success.softwareadvice. com/david-norton-customer-analytics-secrets-1013/.

things David did was have new property hires come to Las Vegas for orientation, both in terms of knowledge and to build relationships.

While the traditional media budgets remained primarily under the control of the properties, David's team handled overall branding and also bought media centrally, to which it sought to apply a performance-oriented mindset. One story David tells relates to launching a new Caesars brand campaign TV spot in Los Angeles. David and his team wanted to be able to spend money on the ad, so they took some of the digital advertising budget in their control to test its impact. Analysis showed there was a significant increase in call volume and web traffic from LA compared to other markets and the company's other brands in LA—in essence, showing there was a positive ROI to traditional advertising spend that was used to secure more budget the following year for traditional advertising to do a national launch. The brand spot was much more productive than direct-response television (DRTV), which was attracting a set of customers that weren't particularly profitable.

At the same time, David built a 100-person marketing team that owned lots of analysis and execution. "We had several of the best breed tools: Teradata, Unica, Cognos, SAS," he says, "and we did the vast proportion of it internally, so we were broadly self-sufficient." This included a very sophisticated direct marketing operation, with a strong understanding of campaign and program profitability. As one might expect for a marketer in an industry that has to know and play the odds carefully, "We were very objective in our judgments; the loser programs went quickly."

By contrast, a common pattern David sees today is for central analytic groups to make big investments in tools and services (SAS or Merkle, for example) but not to match that with an investment in training for the marketers who must leverage the insight, or a commitment and active effort to get their buy-in. In fact, these are really pre-conditions for investing in analysis.

Eventually Harrah's made the decision to move the marketing analytics team under finance. While this had the advantage of adding to the group's critical mass and focus, in David's view it moved the capability too far from the operating units it was supporting. Also, David suggests this was difficult for the members of the team to accept; they had come to see themselves as marketers, too, in terms of their desired career path.

Relationship with IT

David described a very strong relationship, both formal and personal, with Harrah's CIO. Personally, they were "good buddies," as he put it. Formally, their partnership was centered on a steering committee consisting of David (as CMO), the head of finance, and the CIO. This committee met throughout the year to make decisions about how data and technology would evolve to meet the needs of the business, as well as approve and prioritize individual technology projects.

David pointed me to a *MediaPost* article he wrote in 2013[4] that describes this relationship more vividly:

> In my time as CMO of Harrah's/Caesars, my relationship with our CIO was crucial to our success. A staggering percentage of the work we did hinged on turning analytics insights into customer-focused action via technology initiatives. Projects were kicked-off in collaborative work sessions, pitched to the executive team in unison, managed jointly, and celebrated collectively. It did help that the CIO and I skied together, and we formed our bond over fresh California powder. While we challenged each other down the mountain, our best ideas and solutions were often formed on the chair lift ride up. When he

---

[4] David Norton, "CMOs: Buy Your CIOs Lunch; Make It A Regular Date," *MAD Commentary*, MediaPost Blogs, September 30, 2013, http://www.mediapost. com/publications/article/210233/cmos-buy-your-cios-lunch-make-it-a-regular-date.html.

decided to leave, in order to maintain and enhance how Marketing and IT were aligned, his position was filled by someone whom I had hired and who had worked for me for five years. With that change, my CIO "bonding time" moved from the slopes to the coffee shop, but the relationship remained one of my most important in the organization and the positive collaboration continued to strengthen both our teams.

Fortunately for David, from 1994 to 1997 the firm had made a major effort to integrate and consolidate information systems across properties and to create a single data warehouse for analysis of property results. Building off this base, David subsequently integrated slot machine data, customer service data, and CRM data to inform the Service Profit Chain[5] framework that drove Total Rewards. By 1999, David had things in good enough shape that statisticians on his teams could extract and mine data themselves, rather than going through the highly laborious process of ordering data "by the glass" from IT and its source systems.

---

[5] Heskett, James L., Sasser, W. Earl Jr., and Schlesinger, Leonard A., "The Service Profit Chain: How Leading Companies Link Profit and Growth to Loyalty, Satisfaction, and Value," The Free Press, New York, 1997.

Rob Schmults

Vice President, Ecommerce

Talbots

With characteristic modesty, Rob says he "blundered" into the Internet in 1994, helping to grow a pre-Second-Life 3D multi-user environment software vendor from 10 to 100 people. These were the days before the landmark Netscape IPO; Rob recalls trading emails with Yahoo! Founder Jerry Yang to get links to his firm up on that seminal portal. But mostly Rob got blank "What...?" stares in those days when he explained what he did, more he believes because the consumer-facing Internet was so new, rather than because people had a hard time getting their heads around what Worlds, his firm, did. "That was true for pretty much everything on the Internet at that time, even ideas that ultimately broke through."

A Yale grad with an M.Phil. from Cambridge and an MBA from Harvard, Rob followed up his initial entrepreneurial foray with a post-business school stint at McKinsey as an ecommerce specialist. (Rob and I first met in 1999 on an Internet panel discussion at the McKinsey office in Washington, D.C.). There, Rob would field questions like, "Is Amazon really worth what it's worth?" and reply with answers like, "Not by any conventional measure of value; here's what you'd have to believe..." Later, Rob went from being "the Internet guy at a strategy firm to the strategy guy at an Internet firm," at Fort Point Partners. Fort Point, a services firm, was an early pioneer in building advanced ecommerce-oriented sites. The firm later morphed into Offermatica, which was acquired by Omniture and is now at the core of Adobe Test & Target, one of the most widely used digital platform testing solutions in the world. After Fort Point, Rob oversaw a number of ecommerce businesses for GSI Commerce, later held top positions at a variety of digital marketing firms, and also played advisory roles for Shop.org and Bazaarvoice—all before joining Talbots in 2013.

About Talbots

At Hingham, Massachusetts-based Talbots, Rob is just now rowing in to help take ecommerce to the next level. He describes the initial glass as pretty full: The firm has a very loyal customer base, with strong brand affinity and a good feedback loop to the firm itself. The firm is an "omni-channel" marketer, with over 500 physical stores, a house list with nearly 40 million names, and even a private-label credit card with extensive circulation. In his capacity, Rob seeks not only to drive revenues of the Direct segment, but must also support sales within the store network, which like most retailers drives the bulk of sales. (Rob is careful to point out that the conversations we've had reflect his overall views rather than specific strategies and approaches being pursued by Talbots.)

On Finding Opportunities

Rob is not, of course, a women's clothing merchandising expert. Rather, he relies on his extensive experience, organized through a simple framework, to help him decide where he should focus his (and his team's) attention. He describes the conventional silo approach many ecommerce firms take as a "Layer Cake." Each tier represents a major element of a "customer journey." In this model, the layers broadly include Acquisition, Creative, and Site Mechanics (features and functions as well as merchandising). "The issue I see over and over again is firms and their third-party service providers acting like a layer cake, where each operational unit or firm acts like its own, independent layer. So you have OLM (OnLine Marketing, which might actually be multiple layers if SEM, display, affiliates, social are all separately managed), creative, site operations and merchandising, and CRM/eMail all acting relatively autonomously and often not effectively sharing information." The result is potentially a bad customer experience (customers don't expect a layer cake) and pretty much always a sub-optimal one. "So," Rob says, "My own view is—to the greatest degree possible—to eliminate the layer cake phenomenon and have online marketing (OLM), the site, email, customer service, etc. working more as a cohesive whole rather than as separate operating units with different (and potentially) conflicting objectives."

Rob offers the following example: "OLM will often be tasked with top line numbers. Try to get them to focus on profitable traffic, as opposed to just revenue-driving traffic, and you'll hear things like, 'Well, we don't control pricing so we can't be held to bottom line.' The first part is true, but nobody gets to control everything. And if you don't hold OLM to *profitable* traffic, they will logically bring you all sorts of volume that you would be better off *not* having."

Rob continues, "The first thing I do is look *across* the business, both 'customer-experience-in' and 'conversion-data-out.' I use both qualitative and quantitative data to support a higher-level analysis for bigger opportunities. What I've found is that while our customers don't want to work through silos, certain groups will be tempted to play poker with their data to guard their turf. So if you stay at their granular level, you can lose perspective."

Once he's satisfied he's got the balance of focus and effort right at the top level, Rob can dig in to each element. In Acquisition, Rob looks "inside out" (meaning starting lower in the purchase funnel), starting with search, and in particular at the performance of search engine marketing (SEM). One place he focuses is the balance between branded and non-branded keywords. "Branded keywords work," says Rob, "but that's because what you're really doing is simplifying navigation for people who've already decided to buy from you. Non-branded SEM is a lot more work, but here you're targeting people who know what they want—say, a cashmere sweater—but haven't yet decided where to get it."

Rob is particularly wary of averages. For example, an average 15% cost as a percentage of sales on search terms may have a very broad underlying keyword performance distribution, where a few high performers are making up for a long tail of weak performers. One way Rob tries to manage this is to direct his SEM team to manage upper and lower bands. If a keyword group is performing well, say an effective cost per acquisition (eCPA) of less than 10% of each sale, Rob will increase the bid behind it until the eCPA rate moves to or above the lower band—in other words, until he no longer feels there are additional profitable customers that are being left on the table. Conversely, if a keyword group is performing poorly, perhaps above a 20% eCPA, for example, he will reduce support for it, to the point where it either comes back into his desired performance band or drops from the buy altogether. "You can't just consider cost per click (CPC) because the conversion once the visitor hits your site is different, and also the margin on the product may be different. So I think eCPA is the way to go, and then ideally you adjust your eCPA to align with the underlying margin, along with other factors. (Note: This notion of de-averaging can also be extended across multiple dimensions. For example, if you suspect geography is a driver of response to search engine marketing generally for some reason—say, different levels of category or brand awareness in different cities—you may decide to "band-manage" your keyword groups city by city.)

In terms of site mechanics, Rob also warns us to Beware Of The Small Sample. For example, he says, "I'm a big believer in recommendations. But think about how recommendations are arrived at. For a typical site, you start with 100% of traffic. Then 3% convert. Some sliver of that 3% buys product X. Some portion of that sliver that buys product X buys additional products. From that, three of those additional products are bought most frequently. Those products are then shown as recommendations. And that's absolutely the right thing to do as retailer after retailer has found. But we're talking a sliver of a sliver of a sliver of that initial 100%. What if we have a visitor who is more like the person who bought the fourth most common product to be bought with product X? Or the fourteenth? The ones that didn't make the cut *on average* would perform better in that specific case.

So there are often multiple best answers for which recommendation to show; sometime the one that is not the best on average can be more effective. Let's say you're buying your kids a baseball uniform shirt as a present. Yankees shirts may sell best nationally, and therefore be 'most popular.' But if you're in Boston, acting on this recommendation data could be suicidal. Rather, I've found that it's often better to carefully review what recommendations get made by default, and consider whether, subject to the limits of a credible data set, it makes sense to personalize recommendations based on some variable, perhaps like the geography of the visitor."

Executing On Insights

"One thing that's plagued online," says Rob, "is that the people who started this business had to be builders. They literally had to build their stores before they could start selling. That creates a fundamentally different view of roles and responsibilities. For example, if you asked a physical store manager 'How's business?' you'd never hear 'Well, this month we installed new lighting, and the talking price tags go live next month.' They'd be less about pixels and more about stock-out rates in popular sizes." By contrast, ask an ecommerce person what's on deck for next year and they tend to focus on "Design and launch site x or feature y" and less on the performance of what they are operating. This means that time and time again you see insufficient attention given to inventory levels, to basic usability and shopability. A physical store manager is going to raise bloody murder if she's hollowed out on core sizes in core product. She's also going to be absolutely certain her store is easy to get around. The online counterpart all too often gets distracted by shiny keys."

Like others I spoke with, Rob feels that if he's been successful, it's because he's been lucky to have a great relationship with his IT counterparts. In fact, in general he's found that IT executives are better at understanding business issues and requirements than marketing executives are at understanding IT enablers and constraints.

"Businesspeople that allow adversarial relationships with IT to develop...that just can't happen," says Rob. "I've seen that, and it's inexcusable to let it happen." Where it used to be in the early days of ecommerce that "IT just didn't get the web," Rob observes that we've seen a major generational turnover in IT now. "The leaders that didn't get the web have mostly moved on, and the new leaders are seeing they need a more flexible, iterative approach. The advent of labs— think, for example, Walmart Labs—and the shockingly swift adoption of new point of sale (POS) models are good markers for this trend."

Keeping Up

I asked Rob what sources of information he uses to stay informed or to learn more about new ideas. His answer was a refreshing reminder. "If I want to learn about something new, I'll root around to find someone who's trying it too, and call them up! The verbal exchange is usually the most efficient for getting to the heart of it. Plus, you can get lessons learned and pitfalls to watch out for that you won't read anywhere or hear on a stage."

Annemarie Frank

Vice President, Multi-Channel Marketing
HSN

I spoke with Annemarie at the very end of a Friday afternoon, having been introduced by our mutual friend Judy Honig, founder and CEO of the digital strategy consulting firm Lapine Group. I was the last thing standing between Annemarie and the end of her work week, but she couldn't have been more friendly and helpful.

HSN is a $2 billion multi-channel retailer (part of $3 billion+ HSNi, which encompasses a number of other direct specialty retailers), ranking number 24 on the latest *Internet Retailer* "Top 500" list. Annemarie joined HSN two years ago to run digital marketing, after 14 years at American Express and Avon. She described the common thread in her career crisply, noting she has now been part of three transformations of businesses, in each case from a historically dominant analog channel, to the digital realm. Before the web, doing business with American Express happened predominantly through call centers. Avon relied on an iconic direct sales model supported by paper brochures and catalogs. And HSN (formerly Home Shopping Network) depended, eponymously, on broadcasting its shows through television cable networks. Speaking of her transition from her past roles in Manhattan to St. Petersburg, Florida she took particular note of the pace at HSN: "very fast, even by New York City standards!"

One reason for the HSN culture's upbeat tempo might be the unique dynamics of the legacy business model. On television, fixed production costs make airtime a precious commodity. Compounding this, only one product is presented at any given moment. So, as with any anchor on a news, sports, or entertainment show, each of its 22 hosts[6] wears an earpiece to let him or her know how the product being discussed is doing, along with advice about how long to stay

---

[6] http://www.hsn.com/article/show-hosts/3430.

with it and when to move on. The metric is simple, and the feedback is immediate: dollars of sales per minute.

Annemarie points out that online, the challenge is very different, along with the people, processes, and technologies for addressing it. Channel (digital real estate) you can use and merchandise you can present are less constrained. Yes, premium screen space is limited, and product inventories aren't infinite, but there are always more screens, and thus more opportunities to present expanded stocks.

The challenge isn't new, of course; HSN has been online for over 15 years now. Just as with television, it has optimized its marketing efforts for the return on investment in relevant digital marketing channels: display and paid search, email, and, more recently, mobile and social. Over the past year, along with many others, it has begun to move away from a "last-click" approach to optimizing these investments, and it has been evaluating a "full-attribution" model. In this approach it begins, through complex multivariate regression techniques, to try to give appropriate sales influence credit to all of its channels in order to make better decisions about how much to spend on each. Clearly, television and display drive paid search, and all three generate a halo effect that no doubt influences customers' willingness to open up direct mail and email. But how much? While HSN is excited about the potential of this analytic strategy, it has realized that it can be logistically complex to stage the necessary data and align all the execution channels to be able to take advantage of these insights. Also, recently Annemarie and her team have expanded their scope from digital marketing to "omnichannel" marketing, picking up responsibility for direct mail, package inserts, and phone-based programs. This expansion amplifies the potential for properly optimized outreach, but also the analytic challenge. Consequently, as much as the attribution vision is tantalizing, HSN is focusing even more on the roadmap—on picking the right sequence of channels and other factors to add to the model—as its first order of business.

Despite the differences between more-constrained television and less-constrained digital channels, both compete for an equally limited resource: a customer's attention. Accordingly, beyond full attribution there's an even more important analytic transition underway: the evolution from a transactional optimization focus to a customer relationship cultivation perspective. To this end, Chief Marketing and Business Development Officer Bill Brand, whose background is in the media business, has brought a customer experience perspective to marketing investments, with an emphasis that's less on the size and conversion rate of the next visitor's shopping basket than on the lifetime value of each customer in HSN's file.

Along with this has come a focus on driving engagement as much as conversion. "Digital has focused historically on driving the checkout. Now it's more about inspiration," says Annemarie. The changing dynamics of its audiences raise the stakes for this shift. "We can't just rely on translating the strong affinity our customers have for our hosts online. Many of our customers are not watchers of the hosts' shows. For example, take email, where we have some interesting dynamics. Our newer customers aren't as connected to our television programming, so host picks don't influence them as much. So we have to create new experiences to reach these new audiences." And so, HSN has found new ways to partner with celebrities whose product lines it has featured. HSN-produced events are one example, like Mary J. Blige's recent Christmas concert, performed at HSN's studios in St. Petersburg.[7]

With these experiences come incremental production costs, of course. Annemarie admits, "It's still very tricky, especially in such a results-focused environment, to strike the right balance between engagement and conversion. The way forward for us has been through the data." Through a strong partnership with the head of CRM, who

---

[7] Jay Cridlin, "Mary J. Blige Debuts Christmas Album With Concert at HSN in St. Petersburg," *Tampa Bay Times*, November 13, 2013, http://www.tampabay.com/blogs/soundcheck/mary-j-blige-debuts-christmas-album-with-concert-at-hsn-in-st-petersburg/2152238.

also reports to CMO Brand, and a research and analysis team that reports to CAO, HSNi and CFO, HSN Michael Attinella, Annemarie and her team have carefully examined pre-, during-, and post-event (and other promotion) data to assess impacts. They have also deployed other approaches, such as online games; visitors can play anonymously, but need to register to keep "points" they win toward promotional offers for different products. "People who play come significantly more often and stay much longer than non-players," she noted.

Aside from the positive results achieved through experience investments *per se*, Annemarie noted another important dynamic: "Historically, with a focus on each show, or mailing, or campaign, instead of a focus on our customers and their experiences, our options for slotting vendors and their products into these campaigns were more limited, which made negotiations with them more black and white, and therefore challenging. Now, with a better ability to understand customers and how they roll up to relevant segments, and how we might create product assortments and work these into overall experiences for these segments that play out over time, we have more degrees of freedom—more options—for working vendors' products in as well. The customer-oriented data's been really helpful in this regard."

Creating the data infrastructure for this unified view of the customer has been a major focus for HSN over the past year. Working with IBM, the firm has steadily integrated different files—online and direct mail, for example—and has begun to re-model purchase propensities and lifetime value potential in order to inform how much to invest behind various marketing programs. Given the ongoing evolution of its attribution analysis, these models are a work in progress; nonetheless, HSN is already in the field with tests based on the insights they offer.

Also, as for everyone else in the field, recruiting and developing her team is an area of special focus for Annemarie. She explained that she looks for and tries to develop fluency with metric-driven and analytic thinking for her marketing team. While partners can help start and extend this analytic orientation, it's a critical skill to build in-house, as creating objectively-validated customer experiences is at the strategic core of the business. She pays particular attention to a financial orientation: "I ask, 'How in your prior or current role have you evaluated the effectiveness of your programs?' If the answer's not about the bottom line...that's bad."

Judah Phillips

Founder
SMARTCURRENT

Judah Phillips is a widely followed executive, hands-on practitioner, and thought leader in the digital analytics world. Prior to setting up his own consulting firm, SMARTCURRENT, where he works with a portfolio of leading brands on their toughest analytic challenges, he led the web analytics team at Monster.com, the online recruiting service with one of the most trafficked web sites in the world. Judah and I originally got to know each other when he organized the "Web Analytics Wednesdays" series for the Web Analytics Association (now Digital Analytics Association, or DAA). He's the author of *Building A Digital Analytics Organization* and *Digital Analytics Primer*. Judah graciously and patiently spent several hours with me talking about his experiences and sharing his lessons.

Judah got his start in the field working on search. "I started working in software technology in the early 1990s in a space known as 'information retrieval,'" he says—before Google or even eBay existed on the web. "At the time, I was working for a start-up that was productizing an ANSI C (the standard version of the C programming language) toolkit for searching structured and unstructured text, enabling querying of the data, and returning the best passage in a search results list. When modern search engine technology was developing in the late 1990s and early 2000s, I was drawn to learn more about the importance of analytics to a business. I used to work on improving "search engine ranking" before it was called 'SEO.'"

Judah worked mostly with engineers, so he was able to learn the mechanical underpinnings that generate digital data and then start exploring more advanced concepts about search and, later, web server analytics. The start-up was acquired; the dot.com implosion occurred. "I started my own consultancy doing analytics, SEO, and Internet strategy and then, after several years, I wanted to make a change from client-focused work for companies like Sun Microsystems," says Judah. "At the time, it was uncommon to find a full-time job 'doing web analytics' but I was able to find one with an innovative global media company." Within about five years, "web analytics" was increasingly popular, and Judah found himself running a large team of analysts for one of the largest web sites in the world at the time (Monster.com)—analyzing the behavior of tens of millions of visitors and the impact of advertising, like Super Bowl ads, on a website's business. By that point, his skill set had expanded to include much more than just web analytics—from business intelligence to customer analytics to the analysis of both qualitative and quantitative data. "I was developing a solid set of skills for answering business questions from senior executives and line of business executives, and leading analytical teams." Since then, Judah also completed two Master's degrees, continues to advise several startups, speaks at dozens of conferences, contributes to articles, and has authored two books.

"While I've always worked with companies that had a primary emphasis on the internet as the channel for generating revenue, I don't think the basic outlines of a business impact how one does analytics that much," Judah explained. "At the end of the day, there is a customer, in a lifecycle who is activated in a purchasing cycle where there is awareness, favorability, consideration, acquisition, conversion, retention, and loyalty. It's more or less the same if you sell clothes or content." Judah notes that what *is* different is the organization (meaning the people in it), the company's processes, the investment available, the expectations of stakeholders, and the types of emphasis for analytics. "Some companies are more focused on conversion optimization, while others may have larger concerns about branding and awareness or loyalty and retention," he says. "Based on understanding what generates profitable revenue for the business, I make sure stakeholders get answers to their questions and that the business becomes data-informed. That said, there are a lot of ways to describe a customer (such as primary research); however, I tend to use financial metrics and derivative behavioral metrics in the context of cohort analysis (following a group of customers over time and observing how they react to different events)."

We talked about what things typically look like when he's engaged the organizations he's worked with. "I have walked into some well-oiled yet leaky machines, and into companies that had no ability to produce accurate analysis. I was hired to fix, reengineer, or evolve analytics—generally by creating a centralized analytics team and the appropriate team structure, mission, vision, strategy, technology, process, and deliverables." Along with that, Judah notes, he's often asked to define the strategic plan (issues to focus analytic attention on) and the tactical roadmap (how to organize data and people) to execute and then direct it all. "At times, I've even had to project manage it all, too," he adds. "In most companies where I have worked, the marketing team usually looked at data in silos, from their vendor partners, or reports prepared somehow by somebody. In most cases, regardless of the data, I have seen instances where the marketing teams believe this data without having ensured its accuracy or don't believe it and operate off of "gut." At this point in my career, I have very strong feelings that a marketing team can't judge it's own success." Judah has come to strongly believe that any marketing activity or suggested marketing program should be assessed by an unbiased, centralized analytics team who then also does the follow-on evaluation. "In the best of companies, the marketing leadership embraces and adopts this. In the worst-case scenario, it can become political. Good marketers are worth their weight in gold; however, in the Internet business, it takes years to become a good marketer, and so you need an objective way of evaluating whether the ones you have are getting there."

Judah has distilled the lessons he's learned into a vision and roadmap for the analytics capability he describes in his books. In particular, he's defined what he calls the "Analytics Value Chain" and the "Unified Customer Analytics Lifecycle." The Analytics Value Chain, in summary, defines the work an analytics team does. This work generally involves the following process:

- Business requirements and questions

- Data collection

- Data governance

- Analytics

- Reporting

- Optimization and testing

- Prediction

- Automation

While Judah presents these concepts as steps in a linear process to help with comprehension, he acknowledges that the reality is that a team may be working on one, more than one, or all of these things in order of what's important to the business.

These work activities in the Analytics Value Chain enable a company to use their data to reduce cost or increase revenue by measuring the customer lifecycle. Judah describes the Unified Customer Lifecycle as moving from high-order, surveyed concepts (like awareness and favorability) to quantitatively measured concepts, like acquisition and conversion, to measures of retention and loyalty. Through his past observations of customers' purchase lifecycles, Judah's developed his own view of the typical lifecycle he calls the "Tumbler," which recasts the traditional marketing funnel in a more non-linear way.

I asked Judah for examples of wins that he uses as stories to bring his vision to life with his clients. Judah has had many successes in his career helping people understand, with data, what is going on in their businesses. Once he demonstrated that 40% of a firm's marketing spend was being wasted on underperforming channels, because the cost of capital and marginal revenue was not accounted for in their traditional media analysis. "But, if you asked the marketing team, everything was great, when in fact, it wasn't," he says. "Once upon a time I realized after a few hours on a client project that more than $1M per year was being misallocated on mobile paid search."

Another time, he was able to confidently quantify the direct response and branding impact of a Super Bowl ad on a premier Internet site. Also, "I once had to create a cross-domain tracking system that was used to pay a nine-figure revenue share between two publicly traded internet companies. If the analytics weren't correct, then the payments would have been incorrect. All of these projects and programs worked out—the clients claimed real value—so I consider them successful, too," he says.

I asked him where things have proceeded more slowly. He referred to situations where people didn't understand how much organizational change and change management across people, process, and technology was necessary to not only collect data, but to actually analyze it. "In addition, analytics brings transparency. I've always said that if the data doesn't support commonly held beliefs or show positive performance, it will be questioned. Thus, when the analysis doesn't do these things—and in fact does the contrary—things can move more slowly," he observed.

We talked about how he's marked progress towards his vision in his work with clients. I asked whether he's more focused on getting inputs in place or on the insights, actions, and results coming out. He said, "I do monthly newsletters, quarterly business reviews, and usually ask stakeholders for qualitative feedback twice a year. I also am very explicit in identifying the strategic plan for analytics—the timelines for what will be delivered and when it will be delivered—so nothing is a surprise." Of course, *ad hoc* projects and critical issues come up. "I also require that my team (and I as well) use some sort of ticketing system so we can document the work we do as it occurs. That way, I am always prepared if anyone asks 'What is the analytics team doing?' I also have available a deck that describes what the team does, ready to present to anyone who asks at any time."

We also talked about what he's learned about recruiting and developing people, and building analytic organizations. "One thing I can confirm is that no single person can do it all; it takes a team with multiple forms of expertise to make the data sing. The same person who may be good at creating and delivering business analysis is likely not the same person who can implement a logical data model in your BI tool. The same person who writes your tags isn't likely the same person who can query your data warehouse. The same person who builds your data warehouse is likely not the right person to put in front of your CMO to explain analysis. Of course, there are cases, often in smaller companies, where each version of what's needed is more basic, and one person has the right skills to do it all. However, in larger distributed and matrixed global corporations, you need a team. Thus, companies who think they are going to hire one hot shot and top gun—without empowering that person with additional resources and help from different functions—won't be as successful as those who consider creating real teams and understanding that to be "data informed" requires organizational, process, people, capital, and technology changes."

Since building a larger team with many different skills is a large challenge, our conversation turned to relying on vendors for help. "In the end, tools are tools and vendors are vendors, and what they offer as products and services can usually be replaced. The most valuable vendor relationships I have are with the executives of the ones that actually kept watch on their engagements to deliver business value and ensure our success, rather than just delivering the work output we asked for. These were ultimately the ones we kept working with as we built our in-house capabilities, even if the relationship changed."

In an often-political multi-agency context, moving past political agendas to drive decision-making analytically can be a significant challenge. I asked Judah what his experiences with this have been, and how he's done it. "Through honesty and accuracy," he says. "If the facts are with you, it's important to play your role and not back down or be intimidated at all. I provide data-informed analysis that presents what has happened, the business impact, and, perhaps, what you should do as a result. At the end of the day, I am going to tell you what has happened, what is happening, what may happen next and in the future, and what you may want to do about it. The great news is I have the data to back up my assertions and ideas. If somebody disagrees and wants to go in another direction, then okay, let's see how it works out—with data."

Our conversation turned to wrangling access to necessary data, relationships with IT, and how he's divided responsibilities between his analytic teams and what IT groups do. "I have always had positive relationships with IT because I realize that the corporate culture always wins; for analytics to be successful, we need to respect the existing context. What I mean by that is that IT will likely have a way to do things, like request work in Agile sprints or via road-mapping process, so I adhere to those processes and play along in the game. I also always require an allocation of IT resources to do analytics. That allocation can be a matrixed part-time or full-time employee, or it can be an allocation of points in Agile (the software engineering methodology, adapted for other uses[8]) or inclusion in the road mapping and backlog. If I don't get adequate technology support when it is required, then I won't take the client work or job. That said, the level of IT support you need is changing. For example, Tag Management Systems (TMS) have reduced the requirement for IT support to change digital data collection, and the emergence of software-as-a-service (SaaS) coupled with adequate vendor services have changed the dependence an analytics executive has on IT."

As for the thought leaders he follows, Judah mentioned Thomas Davenport, Edward Tukey, Bill Inmon, Ralph Kimball, Bruce Latner, Avinash Kaushik, Justin Cutroni, "and a lot of other folks I named in the Thank You pages for my books." And in terms of his own ideas for where things are headed and what we need to anticipate, Judah noted a final chapter in *Building A Digital Analytics Organization* that covers an extensive range of issues including predictive personalization,

---

[8] "Agile Management," http://en.wikipedia.org/wiki/Agile_management.

closed loop behavioral feedback systems, real-time addressable advertising across multiple screens, sensing and responding, interacting and alerting, geo-specific relevancy and intent targeting, automated services and product delivery, and data interactive shopping experiences. Beyond these concepts, he says, "I am very interested in the mobile customer outside of the traditional funnel—as I've described with the idea of the Tumbler. In a sense, a person with a mobile device is shopping, seeking, and sharing simultaneously. Shopping is related to higher-order mindsets like awareness and favorability, while seeking is about acquisition and conversion, and sharing is about retention and loyalty in social spaces. One doesn't move cleanly to the next; it poses all sorts of interesting analytic challenges to sort out what might happen."

Latham Arneson

Vice President, Interactive Marketing
Paramount Pictures

I first spoke with Latham Arneson on a Saturday morning in January, when he was kind enough to share a few minutes from his weekend. Ms. Perry Hewitt, the Chief Digital Officer at Harvard University and a mutual friend had introduced us. He was in Los Angeles, making fresh-squeezed orange juice while the California sun streamed in his kitchen window; I was in my office in gray, snowy Boston, working on this book. It's possible he was taking pity on me.

Latham currently works at the movie studio Paramount Pictures, but he started his career in a much more traditional tech role at Microsoft working on a (now defunct) website, Windows Live Expo, that aimed to compete with Craigslist. After a swift introduction to the world of tech, he migrated south to LA and joined Paramount's interactive marketing team; in 2008, he was a part of *Fortune* magazine's "Faces of The Future."

In Paramount's context, the interactive marketing formula contains a number of efforts, including an official website for the film, whose launch coincides with the first trailer months before a film is scheduled to open, as well a variety of related promotions in online advertising (display and search), with partners (Fandango and MovieTickets, for example), and through PR and social media. Currently, Paramount executes approximately twelve such campaigns per year. While their primary purpose is to host content, the sites also can act as analytic touchstones and inform on things like overall interest levels, who-is-interested based sources, and characteristics of traffic. However, given the very tight pre-open windows—only a few weeks where major media is spent, typically—opportunities to read trends (social media, web traffic, ticket sales, and so on) and adjust site and advertising creative, along with promotional levels and mix, are limited. And since a film's opening weekend is an incredibly powerful predictor (even, given viral dynamics, a self-fulfilling prophecy) of a film's lifetime performance (well into home media and beyond), once it's out, it's really hard to influence its trajectory.

Analytically, the tight window for insight drives Latham and his team down two paths. First, within each campaign, whatever opportunities might exist to make "reads" must be seized right away: "We really need information on the trailer releases immediately," says Latham. "And," he adds, "of course we need to be cost-effective." This has meant relying on external analytic partners who have well-developed, highly flexible infrastructures (Paramount uses Google Analytics, for example), or unique capabilities, such as Crimson Hexagon (for sophisticated semantic analysis of social media chatter and volume). Second is a focus on what can be learned from each promotional campaign in an overall view—which audiences respond to what approaches—that can be applied to future campaigns. In a sense, given the reasonable number of "reps" (repetitions, or in this case the dozen films released each year) available, each campaign is a test unto itself.

Beyond describing and reporting how well films are generating interest, the analytic "holy grail" is to be able to predict how a film will perform weeks or months *before* release. Today, Latham notes that the strongest correlation for performance is with the number of screens a film opens on. This is a "supply-side" driver of course, itself a function of how well the chains screening films think they will do. A better "demand-side" predictor would help Paramount not only work with theater chains to get the screen count right, but also to pre-arrange its promotional plans more effectively. Accordingly, Latham and his team continue work to support the traditional prediction methods by looking at existing and emerging technologies that may provide significant room for improvement here. One small example we discussed: "Imagine a smartphone app that passively listens to what film trailers are playing in a theater, which after the movie prompts a user to say if you enjoyed the trailer; and, if you'd like to receive more information about the film, a reminder when it releases and an option to share the content right then. Simply by providing users with a simple utility, you could imagine gathering data that could help create models on those stated intentions with subsequent ticket purchase activity. If it grew to a substantial size, you'd have a great indicator very early on of how a film may ultimately perform."

Mohammed Chaara

Director, Corporate Analytics Group

Lenovo

Mohammed (Mo) Chaara and I met last fall at a Big Data conference in Berkeley and quickly discovered shared interests and acquaintances. But for me, these were ultimately only appetizers for learning more about his unique path to his current role as Director of Corporate Analytics for Lenovo.

Mo first thought to apply his undergraduate degree in math and computer science, and a master's degree in statistics and probability, to a career in business. But in the early years of the last decade, "analytics" and "data scientists" weren't as "cool" as they are today (which of course makes his choices even more of a badge of honor). So Mo took a more circuitous route, starting his career on a project developing models for improving the effectiveness of cloud seeding in Nevada and other western states. Apropos of a book on marketing and sales analytics, he was, quite literally, a rainmaker! Later, at a different firm, Mo worked on Department of Defense projects to develop models and algorithms for chemical weapons detection devices. "These were awesome, exciting, very real-life challenges, and I was very proud to have worked on them," he says.

Nonetheless, he continued to follow his interests on the business side and earned an MBA with a focus on financial engineering in 2007. "This was the time that digital business was really roaring back and going mainstream," he notes. With his background, he was especially drawn to web analytics (now more expansively called digital analytics), and he ended up at Comcast Interactive Media, where he led some of their first efforts to apply analytics beyond direct marketing. Later, at Digitas, the digital marketing agency, Mo further developed his Big Data chops, and in particular began to bring analytics to bear on efforts to understand customer experiences. "Historically, marketers relied on lots of primary research, but we were learning how we could combine all sorts of data from different sources to better understand what people were telling us through their actual behaviors," he says.

Eventually he was recruited to Lenovo to direct global experience optimization for their worldwide marketing group. Recently Mo was asked to work with Lenovo's new Chief Analytics Officer, Anthony Volpe, a senior executive from SAS with a Ph.D. in math from Harvard, to stand up a Corporate Analytics group with an even broader portfolio. One of the group's early challenges, that Mo is involved with personally, has been to spot early signals of potentially pervasive quality issues. "We're combining warranty claims data, social media postings, voice-to-text transcripts from call center interactions, survey data, and even log files and other signals from devices our clients allow us to track," says Mo. He adds, "the relevant applications for any valuable indicators that emerge from this extend to all corners of Lenovo, way beyond simply reducing warranty claims, to managing service costs, informing product innovation and design, and driving manufacturing efficiency."

The breadth of sources and scale of relevant data makes this one of the true poster children for the Big Data revolution. Lenovo is a large and prominent user of tools like Hadoop, and with analytics software leader SAS just 10 minutes southwest on I-40 near Raleigh, there's a close partnership and an extensive use of SAS tools on top of the Hadoop-based data store. But the implications of Lenovo's ambitions don't just influence the technical dimension, they also influence the organizational one. Even as it has formed its new Corporate Analytics group to create a critical mass of expertise for exploiting big data, Lenovo has also retained analytic groups in each of its business units. The corporate group is now hiring "analytics ambassadors" to support these groups. The analytics ambassadors each broadly specialize in different functional domains: product, brand, and direct marketing/sales, for example. However, they also each have a primary group they align with, from a relationship management perspective. Mo describes these hires as "mature in their careers, with a strong understanding of business; having significant executive presence, as well as a deep understanding of data science for significant credibility with the analytic community—in short, an upgrade from the traditional concept of the data scientist."

Thus, the resulting hub-and-spoke model drives not only deep subject matter expertise in the core, but also continuity in the connection between the corporate group and each business unit. Responsibility for senior-level relationship management—between the corporate analytics group and the C-levels of each business unit—is shared between the Chief Analytics Officer (Anthony Volpe) and each of the directors (Mo and his counterparts). The CAO also, notably, functions as a hands-on team member of the corporate analytics group, meaning that he is still significantly involved in helping to frame and solve challenges, in addition to his executive responsibilities for organization building, relationship management, and resource allocation.

Mo admits that his group is still trying to strike a balance between developing deep business unit intimacy and simultaneously providing highly specialized skills that supplement what the groups can do for themselves. Inevitably, this balance can't be a perfect one, because resources are limited and needs change. But he also notes that he and his Lenovo colleagues don't expect that organization can solve everything. Rather, they're also relying on staffing their team with people who are especially agile intellectually and comfortable working in dynamic environments with shifting structures and priorities. He observes that this is often not how data scientists, many of whom have grown in academic settings, operate, noting that he knows this first-hand as a former academic trained in such environments. Mo says, "The more I do this, the more I realize my competitive advantage is not in the specialized skills I learned as an academic; it's the ability to define and solve problems in a fast, dynamic environment, and to that end, to come up to speed quickly on a variety of analytic techniques and know when I need extra help."

One key aspect of defining problems to solve is framing them in languages and terms that are familiar to managers who will use the insights his analytic efforts generate. Mo is sensitive to making sure he's got a good read on how people think as he packages his work. "The McKinsey customer journey model is popular here," he relates. "So we try to understand that model and present our findings in the context it offers for communicating them. Of course no such framework is perfect. If it's too linear—let's say if potential customers actually bounce back and forth between phases of a journey, instead of proceeding inexorably forward—you need to account for that [for example, by using a visitor-based conversion rate calculation, rather than one based on each visit]. That's OK as long as you don't feel you are compromising what the data are telling you in order to fit to the framework. In any event, no one I've ever known has proven their customer journey model is perfectly accurate. I think it's more a philosophy, a means of packaging things. If you're a product-centric company, or a strategy-centric company, it's a way of making sure people see things through different lenses from the ones they're used to."

Another key to effective analytic capabilities is a good model for how to engage IT. Mo suggests a three-tier "analytic maturity" model that he has used to guide his work. In the first stage, the lowest level of maturity, he's had to prove the value of analyzing a particular opportunity. At this stage he stays close to the business, working with the data they've either already got or have access to through existing permissions. "I actually avoid contact with IT at this stage," he says. "They're typically very resource-constrained, and there's no sense in having them spend scarce cycles on planning to manage scenarios that may not go anywhere after we explore them." At the second level, mid-maturity, based on the samples of data used to that point, Mo is able to develop a feel for the data management and governance challenges that will be involved in using the relevant data on a regular basis. For example, there may be master data hierarchies or privacy issues to manage, or quality and completeness checks that will have to be done as part of any regular "extract-transform-load" (ETL) process. Once he's got a clear idea of what kind of management the necessary data will require to support ongoing operationalization of an insight (such as the inclusion of machine signals in the quality prediction model he described) he brings in IT to review what will be required to make it all work.

"Ironically," he notes, "things are usually approached the opposite way." He adds, illustrating with examples from his past experience, "An analytic project starts with foundational thinking about the universe of data that might be used for a class of analysis, and how it might be physically and logically governed and defined. The problem is that nine months later, you have nothing to show for it, in terms of any business insight or result." So, he continues, "Start with the data you have. Any good analyst can extract value from dirty, incomplete data, at least enough to get a sense for whether there's value worth pursuing further."

Mo noted that his preferred approach for developing analytic maturity can be a tricky one. There's a tendency to want to develop a shadow IT organization that selects and maintains its own tools and infrastructure. Mo feels that this is generally a mistake. In his view, a good analytics group focuses on requirements and stays tool-agnostic as long as what's provided meets the important needs. This is important as a means of avoiding extra overhead that can reduce an analytic team's flexibility to shift course and pursue new capabilities as they appear. For example, if you're committed to a legacy business intelligence (BI) stack, it's harder to reach out to a new Big Data/NoSQL stack that might represent a threat to that. Plus, he notes that the team's credibility is its most important asset, and this comes from being able to be as objective and agile as possible in pursuit of good answers, and, again, carrying a big IT commitment on its back hinders this.

How far into execution and implementation does his team range, I asked? Mo noted that his group generally handles two kinds of requests. Some are *ad hoc* analytic inquiries in which someone (usually very senior) wants an answer to a specific question. In this case, the team's role is quite narrow. But there are also "chartered, strategic" initiatives he and his colleagues pursue (such as the "pervasive quality issues" sensing initiative he described) in which their charge is to go all the way from exploring data for insights to standing up the platforms through which the opportunity will be realized. Generally this means being comprehensively involved at least through an operational pilot, in order to shake out all the bugs in practice. He describes this expansive role for the analyst as "the beginning of a new way of business management, where an analytics team leads the development of solutions that drive strategy," in contrast with a traditional 'executioner-led' model in which analysts are at best silo'd high priests, and at worst simply reporting for a model that may or may not have any business logic for it.

Belinda Lang

Belinda Lang Consulting

Former Vice President, Brand, Advertising, Digital, and

Consumer Marketing

Aetna

I spoke with Belinda on the eve of a week where she would lead three agency reviews—a crushing load by any normal standard, but reasonably routine for her. Despite the prospect, Belinda, to whom I was introduced by our mutual friend Judy Honig, CEO of Lapine Group, never once rushed our conversation; she was the soul of patience and generosity as we talked about her career and what she's learned from it. As you'll see, her experiences have cut across marketing and technology, analysis and operations, and the challenges of getting operations launched but then scaling them in large organizations with lots of pre-existing momentum behind other things. In short, Belinda's the very embodiment of the "analytic marketer" this book suggests as a model for the future.

Today, Belinda, as part of her consulting practice, is a senior marketing advisor for Memorial Sloan Kettering Cancer Center in New York. Most recently, she spent several years leading consumer marketing for Aetna, where she managed an award-winning re-launch of the firm's brand strategy and identity. Before Aetna, she spent over twenty years at American Express (Amex), in a variety of increasingly senior roles she describes modestly as "intrapreneurial," but which all represented significant innovations and in many cases broke open important new sources of growth for the firm.

Her path to these roles, however, was unlikely and unique. "I was an art history major in college [at McGill]," she says. "It may seem paradoxical that later in my career I managed a team of over fifty statisticians at Amex, but you learn research really well as an art history major. You have to pull a number of sources together, each with their flaws, and make judgments; it teaches you a lot about decision making under uncertainty." Considering medical school, she followed up with a master's degree in occupational therapy from Columbia, and then an MBA from NYU's Stern School, both with honors. "I started by thinking I would go into occupational therapy for burn patients, teaching them how to use their hands again," she said, "but as it turns out, I was spending a lot of time on management, marketing, and fundraising for the clinic, and I got pulled toward business—a big piece of being effective in health care is understanding how to make this side of it work."

At the time, American Express was exploring offering its services to health care providers—enabling them to accept payment via the American Express card, to improve their cash flow and reduce risk—and recruited Belinda out of business school to help start that business. "I was a career-changer, but I saw my multiple experiences in working in health care, both as clinician and manager, as the way to market myself. I started at American Express as an intern. It was a wonderful opportunity to be entrepreneurial with the support of a big company, and I was impressed that the executives who recruited me admitted they didn't know much yet about the sector, which at the time was starting an era of significant change, and were willing to hear what I had to say."

The first order of business, which became a recurring point of departure in her work, was to segment the target customer base into relevant groups for the purpose of service design. "Selling our services to hospitals, for example, was very different from selling it to small physician practices in what was then a highly fragmented market. In 1984, a hospital might have wanted to introduce alternative payment mechanisms that would appeal to its patients—in this case, expanding beyond international health care "tourists" for whom paying in cash or by check might be problematic for one side or the other—but hospitals had more sophisticated reporting requirements." On the other hand, the logistics of supporting a small physician's practice might be less complex, but style and nuance is everything here for professionals who in many cases are very uncomfortable talking about payment with their patients. "We had to re-design the Amex point-of-sale (POS) experience to be appropriate for this context," she says, "and 'tip amount' definitely had to come off the charge slip." The segmentation helped to frame and then simplify senior level discussions about how to adjust and manage its business model for the different groups.

Another important lesson learned in these early days in her career was the need to match attention to marketing and sales operations to the analytic insights she was generating about whom to target and how. "Take sales incentives," she says. "We had to lobby to get people to sell to this new class of 'merchants' in their territories, and we had to work the incentive system to get this support. That took us upstream, to design a lead qualification program for smaller offices, which was challenging because at the time Amex required an in-person due diligence visit to a prospective merchant before they could enroll in our program. And, qualifying a doctor's practice is different in many ways from vetting a restaurant."

The program, with its significant cash flow benefits for providers, was a great success. And so Belinda, with her reputation growing for operating effectively in uncharted territories, began a string of high-profile explorations and launches. She joined the Optima card[9] team shortly after its inaugural mailing, and "got involved in everything from there." Afterward, she was recruited by Abby Kohnstamm (who then headed card member marketing for Amex and later was CMO at IBM) to lead the American Express strategy and programs for the "mature market segment." These were pre-retiree business people of the boomer generation who tended to give up their American Express cards when they saw the end of their working days approach, having mentally assigned Amex to the business charges compartment in their "share of wallet" thinking. Once again Belinda brought careful

---

[9] Amex's first credit card offering allowing payment over time, as distinguished from the pay-in-full-each-month charge card.

customer segmentation to bear here, which led to a number of fairly radical innovations, ranging from titling such customers (many from "The Greatest Generation") as "senior members," a special package of card fee discounts, creation of a "senior member advisory board" to take service design input, and launching a set of leisure travel-related marketing offers for this group. "Tuning this program to get the promotional level right—enough to stem attrition, but not so much that we were cannibalizing the cohort that would have stayed anyway—was a highly sophisticated combination of statistical modeling using card member usage data and testing via direct mail. In the end, we were able to cut attrition in half during the first year of the program," she says. Later she was asked by Anne Busquet, another senior Amex executive (later CEO of IAC's local media business and now a Pitney Bowes Board member) to expand the Membership Miles program into a broader range of relevant benefits (and thus merchants) via the Membership Rewards program, which today is widely regarded as the standard among loyalty management programs. The breadth of this effort was significant, extending to branding, structuring of the program, financial modeling, and selling in the partners.

Soon after, she was asked by Phillip Riese, then president of American Express' Consumer Card Group, to figure out, as she puts it, "How do we move out of direct mail?" For anyone with an understanding of the acquisition end of American Express' business, it's clear how significant a challenge this was. Each of the over 100 million incoming calls per year represented a cross-sell opportunity for the highly effective live channel. And of course, electronic media (like email) held the promise of extraordinarily low marginal costs. However, American Express and others in its industry faced legal restrictions on over-contacting potential customers. Even if an individual business unit exercised restraint, the sum of solicitations from multiple units could potentially have put Amex over the limit and subjected it to millions of dollars of fines. The key to managing this, then, was to create a unified customer master file across different business lines and use this in the inbound context in a way that prioritized which offer would be presented in what order, and with what timing, to comply with relevant laws.

Creating such a capability was sufficiently challenging, not only technically but also politically, that Belinda decided to enlist an outside firm to build the file. And in order to further tip the scales in her favor, Belinda at the same time moved to launch a "customer-focused sales" program that would piggy-back offers of relevant services to qualified customers on to service calls. Trying to sell on the tail end of a service call represented a radical cultural shift for an organization famous for its dedication to high-quality service. So, naturally, Belinda pursued an approach based on pilots and tests. "In order to route the calls to the pilots, we bootstrapped a database of products and services different members were eligible for. When a call came in from a member that we thought would be a good prospect for cross-selling a particular thing based on this data, we would route it to the pilot team. We had trained the team in consultative selling approaches and also implemented systems for tracking employee and customer satisfaction. In just three months, we had a fabulous success on our hands. And our models suggested there was enormous untapped potential for the program—so huge, in fact, that in our presentations about it we cut our estimates by 75% because we thought no one would believe us. But then everyone got on board, to the point where even HR was building models to better predict which service reps would be better at cross-selling."

In particular, through these experiences she learned how to interact with IT effectively, summing up that she learned that "IT will respect you as a marketer if you're willing to dig in and understand how things work; in many cases IT professionals are teachers by nature and like to work with folks who have natural curiosity and who like to learn. Also, they'll appreciate you more if you leave room for them to bring their expertise to bear on analytic questions or service design possibilities." She notes, "Unfortunately these characteristics tend to be blind spots for many marketers, who either are not as curious about how technology works or not as flexible to permit tinkering with their visions about how a service or campaign might work in ways that might be more feasible or cost-effective based on technological capabilities and constraints."

Belinda was successful enough in bridging the business-IT gap in these initiatives that eventually she was asked to be the US relationship manager for Amex's Information Management organization, a role she held for four years. Her scope of responsibilities there included managing an analytics team that numbered 40 statisticians as well as other related data access roles. Her vision was to partner closely with business units to leverage data and technology into higher business results, including building models and programs based on their insights. But ironically, her shift organizationally initially carried with it a "tribal" burden. Belinda observes that at times it felt like she worked at a completely different firm, with its own culture and norms. So she undertook a sales campaign in the form of a training program on when to involve her group. Counter-intuitively, however, she emphasized self-service capabilities and skills for business users, rather than "pushing" to get her team involved early in her business partners' efforts, essentially reversing the typical approach most supporting functions take to promoting themselves.

Eventually, though, Belinda decided to seek opportunities back on the business side. "Even though I had developed a very non-traditional skill set around doing everything it takes to get new ventures launched and scaled, I'm a marketer at heart," she says. So she worked her way back toward her passion, landing as the liaison between the global advertising group and the consumer card group. In 2007, she led the development of the American Express Members' Project, the first program to crowd source suggestions from card members and others for directing the firm's charitable giving. The program won awards and was the model for a number of similar efforts by other firms, including the recent and prominent Pepsi Refresh Project.[10]

---

[10] http://en.wikipedia.org/wiki/Pepsi_Refresh_Project.

In 2010, Belinda joined Aetna as the CMO for consumer market-ing, with a charter to build up that function. Here the challenges were different. Aetna had a very well developed B2B sales and marketing capability, but less presence and experience on the B2C side. With-out as much of a pre-existing engine in place, she shifted into a more "builder"-oriented role. This involved a major re-launch of the brand and an advertising campaign to go with it, as well as implementing all the brand tracking capabilities (centered on Net Promoter Score), and bringing on digital and other agencies.

One area of career lessons she particularly focused on in our con-versation was the profile of the kind of person she believes will be successful in the marketing discipline going forward. Citing David Norton as an example, whom she recruited out of MBNA to work with her and who later went on to the CMO role at Harrah's (and who also kindly spoke with me for this book), she mentioned "analytical" and "entrepreneurial" as critical attributes. "You have to have people who don't just think in terms of analysis *or* execution, you have to see them both as part of a seamless, continuous whole," she says. "Also, you don't need to have 100% analytic certainty to act, and you need to be open to new data that might change your direction." Belinda looks for people who blend creativity, analytic acuity, and practicality: "a good combination of left brain, right brain thinking." Finally, "There's a dilemma," she says. "As people get more senior, they tend to hedge their bets on things to work on, because they fear they'll get burned if they do great work on something new but it doesn't launch." She adds, "You have to look for folks who are willing to take the plunge, not just without knowing whether they can get an 'A,' but without knowing how the 'A' will be defined."

Thomas White

Senior Vice President, Institutional Marketing

TIAA-CREF

Thomas White is the Senior Vice President for Institutional Marketing at TIAA-CREF, reporting to Connie Weaver, the firm's Chief Marketing Officer. TIAA-CREF (www.tiaa-cref.org) is a national financial services organization with over $500 billion in assets under management (as of this writing), making it one of the largest such organizations in the world, and it is the leading provider of retirement services in the academic, research, medical, and cultural fields.

In TIAA-CREF's business, the firm must market and sell not only to the organizations that sponsor retirement plans, but also to the individuals who must then decide to participate, by deferring a portion of their income and investing those savings in the investment options offered under the plans. The scope of Thomas' institutional marketing responsibilities extends to what he describes as "B2B2C," which is to say, both of these aspects. As Thomas described it, this includes everything from product development, to packaging and promoting the firm's offerings through multiple channels, starting at the brand awareness and preference levels, moving through the B2B targeting and sales stages (including Request For Proposal, or "RFP" stage), as well as building and managing relationships with the individual participants in the plans the firm manages for their sponsors. The breadth of this challenge, and the associated analytic range, made his a uniquely interesting story for this book.

After getting an undergraduate degree in journalism and a master's in English, Thomas initially thought he'd pursue a career as a reporter. Along the way, however, he interviewed for a job with Fidelity Investments in Dallas, and after six months as a call center service and sales representative, was invited to participate in a management training program that gave him much broader exposure to the firm's operations, including the sales and marketing functions. Finding the latter especially fascinating, Thomas embarked on a career in marketing that spanned both the client and agency side, within financial services and beyond to other sectors, across strategic, direct-to-consumer, and digital aspects of the discipline. But he always found himself drawn to the unique challenges of marketing in financial services, and so has planted his flag there over the last decade.

TIAA-CREF's channel mix is highly varied. It extends from traditional brand-oriented channels, such as television, print, and radio to classic and digital channels such as direct mail, email, display, search and mobile advertising, social media, and even to digital and live interactions through the firm's web sites and call centers. Digital marketing is a large and growing part of this mix of course. Along with this, "Data's very important here," says Thomas. "We're a non-profit, and our charter is to maximize retirement payouts to our participants. So, our metrics are very focused on these outcomes," he adds. "In particular, we're focused on how much of our participants' income they'll be able to replace in retirement."

A central insight from the firm's considerable investment in studying what drives this outcome has been the importance of getting advice. Participants who interact with the firm to get advice, whether through automated or human channels, have much higher activity on virtually every aspect of potential engagement, ranging from enrollment to income deferral (savings) rates through to appropriate asset allocation, and even to other aspects of their financial planning beyond the employer-sponsored plan. Accordingly, Thomas and his colleagues, partnering with the firm's analytic team (which is a peer within the marketing organization, reporting to the CMO) have studied the effect of advice provided through different combinations of channels.

Armed with insights from this analysis, they apply what they've learned to fine tune what combinations are offered to which participants. While digital channels are of course much less expensive, one important dynamic has been that the incremental information gathered through "high-touch" interactions has produced not only higher participant activity rates, but also better outcomes. Sometimes this information is applied at the point of contact—in a single advice conversation, on a phone call or in a live or online workshop, for example. But it's also used for very fine-grained, highly personalized communications to participants. "We do start with broad segmentations to start the conversations," Thomas says. "For example, we can generalize with a Maslow's hierarchy and say that our younger participants will prefer digital and social media channels, and that their educational debt may be top-of-mind for them. Also, we get data from the plan sponsor that helps us with this, such as age, gender, role, compensation, and tenure, and of course we purchase some additional data to help us further...But through our interactions with people, we learn about life events—marriage, children, divorce, etc.—that serve as triggers for addressing relevant concerns. In sum, we learn over 100 different things that we can really only gather through this channel, which then of course multiplies the range of channels and messages we may need to use to reach and help them most effectively."

The power of advice interactions puts a premium on building relationships with participants that increase their interest in having those conversations. This has taken TIAA-CREF's participant communications programs in some interesting directions that are highly innovative within the sector. One successful format has been a competition organized among different organizations under a single plan sponsor's umbrella—in one example, among various Cal Tech faculties and research centers, including its famous Jet Propulsion Lab (JPL)—for the highest enrollments and deferral rates in the Cal Tech-sponsored program. Thomas reports performance on these metrics has gone up "significantly" year on year as a result of this campaign.

Another benefit of the unique data gathered during advice sessions accrues to plan sponsors (the organizations that set up plans for their employees and then contract with firms like TIAA-CREF to administer them). Through this data, TIAA-CREF is able to provide better reporting to sponsors on how well the plan designs, investments, and employee engagement programs they have selected to include in their retirement benefit programs are performing. At the margin, advantages like this are one reason why TIAA-CREF has 70% of the higher education market.

Beyond using the raw information it gathers as mechanical triggers to shape its communications with participants, TIAA-CREF uses models to target all of its products and most of its services. Because of the unique aspects of the data it collects and some inevitable legacy aspects of how data is accessed, while the firm does get help from some outside partners, most of the modeling work is done in-house. Accordingly, customer analytics is organized as a separate center of excellence within the marketing organization, as noted above. At TIAA-CREF, data enablement (the organization, staging, and governance of data) is organized as part of the IT and Operations organization, but Thomas describes a high degree of collaboration across all three separate groups: his teams, the Customer Analytics team, and the data enablement group. "We're very comfortable with analytics," he says. "We use a strategic, end-to-end perspective on our participants' experiences that includes both behavioral and attitudinal data, to ground ourselves and identify subsets of behavior that we can focus on. So, our organizational model for this works fairly well," he adds.

Thomas' charter extends so broadly, across so many different functions—creative services, operations, as well as integration of analytic insights—that he has found it especially important to emphasize common cultural denominators in his recruiting and development efforts. "Being entrepreneurial is important here to getting things done, but being collaborative is much more so. Individual contributions are generally unsuccessful and not rewarded per se; it's really the result of the team effort we're focused on. This is especially important because in the end it's the customer's perspective and outcome that matters here, not some locally-optimized efficiency outcome."

Perry Hewitt

Chief Digital Officer
Harvard University

Perry described Harvard's situation as both having an established brand but also very much operating as a startup in the digital domain whose developing presences there would play an ever-increasing role in all interactions with its constituents.

Like many organizations, one challenge it faces in adapting to this is, paradoxically, a source of its strength in its existing environment. This is Harvard's famously decentralized structure, where budgets and decision-making authority are largely vested in individual schools. In fact, funding for central administrative functions is less allocated from the top and more collected as an overhead charge to the different schools and other entities. This of course makes leading from the center a grand influence challenge. Nonetheless, the good news in this case is the acceptance by the schools of the magnitude of the challenge before them collectively, and a willingness to embrace a shared digital vision for how to address it.

"Back in 2009," Perry said, "there was a more qualitative assessment of digital effectiveness, in part tied to a culture of deference to seniority" (in other settings referred to as the "HIPPO," web analytics guru Avinash Kaushik's term for the "highest paid person's opinion"). "People were less aware of the kinds of analytics we could glean from our digital properties, and therefore the analytics were less central to decisions." Collecting and, even more so, sharing data on digital performance was an enormous cultural shift. "Some had anxieties about it," Perry said, adding, "but we overcame it through transparency. The more open we were with data on the properties we managed directly, the more that came back from our counterparts at the schools. Also, teaching each other was a big part of the exchange; the more we shared best practices, the less fear there was about our 'lessons learned' showing up somehow."

Another ongoing reality was that up until the last few years, analytics were mostly IT-focused (for example, information about uptime, created by server administrators for their bosses). "We used Google Analytics and real-time tools like Chartbeat for a couple of reasons," Perry explained. "First, we wanted to make our deployment as simple and inexpensive and easily accessible as possible. Second, we wanted to make it as relevant and relatable as we could. When we showed Chartbeat to one of the deans, and explained that it was literally a real-time reflection about how his constituents were interacting with a news announcement, it took a while before we could peel him away from it. He kept looking and trying to explain what might be driving the usage patterns and thinking ahead to what the editorial implications might be."

Perry was candid, however, about the time this took: close to two years. One advantage Perry and her colleagues did have was their control of the university's home page and main news vehicle, the *Harvard Gazette*. Her span also extended to the main social media presences, which the data revealed were powerful drivers of traffic to the schools. With this currency clearly accounted for, Perry was able to arrange for two-way data sharing and, later, the application of improved digital operating practices in exchange for ongoing efforts by the center to augment vital traffic.

Given Harvard's prestigious, aspirational positioning, the objectives for its digital properties went well beyond traditional alumni outreach (much of which is still conducted offline through direct channels) and ran more to collecting and conveying stories about the development and application of Harvard's wide variety of offerings. This collection went well beyond internal sources to an engagement, in several specific ways, with the university's global audiences. This in turn had very significant implications for the reach and timeliness of analytic instrumentation and data collection associated with these presences.

Accordingly, the university had to be very thoughtful about what to launch and how to launch it. "Our biggest success story," Perry remarked, "was not what we launched, but what we didn't. And data was a big way we did this. We would start by presenting whatever data we had on comparable properties, as a way of imposing some objective discipline on what it would take for us to stand up and support something that would be competitive. And when we did that, more often than not, if the idea did go further, we could roll it into something that we'd already put up and had the resources and experience to maintain. Also, by focusing our investments, this practice simplified our own delivery and support efforts, improving our service levels to our own and to the schools' and research centers' properties."

This secondary benefit was very important because capable and experienced digital communications specialists are in short supply and are very expensive. So Perry implemented two practices. One was indefatigable networking through a variety of sector- and functionally-relevant associations and other organizations in order to maximize not only the pool of candidates met but also to play up the story of the university's successful expansion into digital channels. The second was to focus less on home run redesigns and more on incremental improvements revealed through close attention to analytics. This latter practice not only better disciplined investments but also helped to build the confidence of her team and helped advance its development in a very substantive, objective way.

To tackle analytics, Perry stayed away from the common practice of outsourcing both implementation and ongoing measurement to a large agency. Rather, she turned to a leading independent analytical consultant to help set strategy and to bring, periodically, a set of fresh, objective eyes to evaluating results. At the same time, she leverages these interactions to help further build in-house abilities to read and react to the data that emerges.

As for building the essential relationship with IT, Perry has part-nered effectively to build analytic capabilities there with a set of shared projects, including a web publishing initiative to advance use of a shared platform: "We learn by using the data together to improve the result." This has made it easier to avoid struggles over control and associated budgets. "When we are driving to a common outcome that we're both accountable for, those arguments become more disagree-ments about means than ends, and we can work through those."

Todd Purcell

Senior Manager, EY Financial Advisory
Customer Experience Practice
Former VP, Digital Strategy, Capabilities & Insights at The Hartford

Todd Purcell's career has blended the breadth of many senior digital marketing roles and the depth of staying focused on a single industry—financial services—throughout. As with many curious, integrative thinkers, focus was initially a challenge. After graduating from Cornell and landing a sales job at Xerox, he quickly realized he wanted exposure to more aspects of business beyond that role. "I was like Michael J. Fox," he laughs, referring to the character Alex Keaton in the '80s sitcom *Family Ties*. "I really wanted to be a businessman. I had no idea what that was, but that's what I wanted."

At Fordham for his MBA, Todd had an epiphany during a class on marketing in financial services. "This was it," he recalls, saying, "I loved the complexity of it, the challenge of communicating effectively for an important set of needs." His first job out of business school was in the bank-training program at then-Chemical Bank, soon to be Chase. "I ended up in the retail business, doing deposit product management for several years, really learning marketing from the ground up. It was a classic bank job, in a central group doing regular rotations to get exposed to different aspects of the retail business." During this span, his work extended to building models for direct mail acquisition efforts, which got him early experience working with data and databases in a hands-on way.

Fate intruded. "My manager said the bank was phasing out a dial-up banking program called Spectrum and moving to Internet banking, and that I should look at that. It turned out to be a classic case of right place, right time for me. It was a great opportunity; I had a small team, we got to work with a lot of different functions in operations and IT." In addition to sorting out the product offering itself, Todd's team had to put together a marketing campaign that included TV, radio, and print to drive people to it.

After a while, Todd observed that the world was getting turned upside down around him by new online channels, and, seeking more responsibility, he moved over to American Express. The opportunity there was to work with a "pure" interactive group, at the center of Amex, charged with developing digital capabilities and experiences for the different groups. Among the things he and his team developed there were services driven by alerts, personalization, and profiling, unified through a "real-time decision engine" to make sure the right content was presented to the right person at the right time. Over time, his responsibilities grew to leading the firm's efforts to provide "off-dot-com" digital channel services, including email, mobile, and SMS-based marketing programs to various business groups. "It wasn't necessarily the most logical scope, because there's so much interdependence between these channels and the web sites. But sometimes organizational needs—like recognizing a young guy's passion and giving him some land to farm—trump logic." One of the consequences, he notes, is that "experiences can have a tendency to be realized and managed in silos. It was a bit blurry."

Eventually, Todd began to have thoughts of trying life beyond financial services, but Smith Barney asked him to help them build "myFi," its all-in-one online wealth management program (analogous to services like Mint.com) for clients with low-six-figure portfolios. "We had an altruistic, aggressive agenda," he recalls. The service was promoted and maintained through social media, including a peer community Smith-Barney set up and maintained, giving Todd a chance to get exposed to this end of the digital marketing spectrum also.

With the 2008 financial crisis and Citibank's sale of Smith Barney to Morgan Stanley, one door closed for Todd and another one opened: the opportunity to run digital marketing for USAA in San Antonio. "This job gave me the opportunity to own all the usual channels: SEM, SEO, Display, email." Historically, USAA had been a big direct mail shop, also relying on word of mouth among its devoted base of customers in the armed services. Now, seeing an opportunity in 2009 to take advantage of its financially sound position, the firm wanted to broaden its outreach to the families of service members, and it made a significant push beyond its traditional marketing channels into TV, radio, and print with its "Big Red" campaign.

Todd's job was to use digital channels to fully harvest the awareness created by the campaign. We talked about the analytic frame he brought to the job. "Basically, USAA has high expectations, not just for the service it provides its members, but also for the performance it gets from the marketing resources it allocates," he says. "So, with the visibility of the Big Red campaign, we had to deliver, and quickly, on the digital front. Really, this sense of urgency is one of the reasons they're so successful."

Two levers seemed especially relevant: email and non-branded SEM. In the case of email, the strong pre-existing loyalty of its members represented a built-in booster for that channel's performance that would make it an especially efficient channel. And, given the air cover from the brand campaign, paid search offered an especially effective way to harvest any near-term market demand. Todd's rallying cry for the search team was "First page or bust!" However, despite the push, USAA still found itself at a spending disadvantage versus firms like Progressive and GEICO, and so Todd needed to rethink USAA's content and tagging strategy to fully gear the media spend. In particular, expanding and optimizing landing pages came into focus. Before, the firm had used "a single front door," as Todd put it; now, Todd brought his Amex experience with profile-based real-time decision engines to bear. Testing, in real-time (in campaign), was also a central feature for both emails and the SEM/landing page programs.

For family reasons, Todd next headed back northeast to The Hartford to assume a role as VP, Digital Strategy, Capabilities, and Insights. Here the challenge was different. Todd notes that for a leader of an analytics function, it's very important to read the core pace of an organization. Some thrive on momentum, placing confidence in leaders that can get things done and keep things moving, even if they aren't exactly the right things. In others, patience and deliberation, and being right are more valued characteristics. As noted elsewhere in the book, these cultural traits—the accumulated weight of past experiences and their consequences—are stronger influencers of behavior than external pressures or executive direction of the moment. At The Hartford, Todd observed that reading peers effectively and building a story that everyone could buy into was more effective for getting things done than driving for short-term action, even if developing and communicating that story took months rather than weeks.

At USAA, Todd's span of control over the execution arm of marketing was fairly broad, with direct reports to him for each of the social media marketing, mobile marketing, and "Demand Generation" (including SEO, SEM, Paid Display, on site personalization, and email marketing). But if you want to move quickly, a strong partnership with organizational units that control the necessary data for executing and analyzing your work is crucial. Todd says, "I've always worked closely with the analytics guys, but at USAA, that was even more important. There, they were a peer to my group, with both of us reporting to the CMO. The relationship was a bit unusual in that they were supposed to play as much of an independent assessment role for senior management as they were an enabling role for our group. Partly this built-in objectivity was how USAA was able to remain successful even as it pushed aggressively into its expansion plan. The tradeoff was that new analytic techniques, such as full attribution, may have been pressed forward faster than the marketing groups could absorb the insights from them. But I connected as tightly as I could with them knowing the importance of their ongoing support, advice, and thought leadership, and I didn't experience any issues in getting the right level of support from them."

Later, at The Hartford, Todd had direct reports for each of his "Connected Customer Experience," "Insights," "Strategy and

Planning," and "Capabilities" groups. This included the digital analytics function, which as a shared service was organized and managed as a Center Of Excellence. One of Todd's main areas of emphasis for this group was to prune back conventional reporting and push for insights. In fact, the change of his group's name (adding "Insights") was a way of reinforcing this expectation. Alongside that symbolic change came a re-evaluation and development of the consultative and relationship skills of the analysts on his teams. "During this time, there was a big push at The Hartford to do more with 'Big Data,'" says Todd. "I may have been a bit myopic, but my emphasis was on doing more with what we had—not just delivering an enterprise-wide reporting capability, but thinking about identifying needs, developing solutions, and then monitoring the data to effectively leverage our efforts beyond the initial look. We needed to make sure the organization could absorb that before expanding the scope of what we looked at. Ultimately, of course we want to tap all relevant online and offline sources to create the connected, seamless customer experiences we're after, but a good analytics organization doesn't stop at designing those on paper. You have to be a partner and share ownership in bringing them to life—that's as much of the analytic capability as anything else."

Ben Clark

Director of Software Development
Wayfair

Online home furnishings retailer Wayfair is white hot, with nearly $1 billion in revenue during 2013, up over 50% from the prior year.[11] Wayfair has reached this position through a strategy of merchandising a very broad selection of products and complementing this selection with a highly sophisticated approach to recommending products shoppers might like as they browse through Wayfair's offerings. Ben Clark is a veteran ecommerce software architect whom I originally met over a decade ago; Ben now leads the Wayfair engineering team responsible for several crucial customer-facing capabilities, including on-site search, recommendations, and specialized sites for events such as flash sales. We sat down recently on a snowy February morning at Pavement, the indie coffee shop near Boston's Symphony Hall and just a couple of blocks from Wayfair's global headquarters, and Ben graciously and patiently offered some insights into how he and his colleagues find and execute opportunities at the very edge of today's analytics envelope.

A September 2012 article in *Information Week*, "Online Retailer Uses DNA Research To Connect With Customers,"[12] offers a glimpse of how far Ben and his colleagues at Wayfair have advanced. It describes how one of Ben's team members came upon a Dutch bioinformatician's application of Markov-chain-based statistical techniques[13] for identifying meaningful clusters in collections of proteins.

[11] Curt Woodward, "$2B Wayfair Valuation A Big Statement in Winner-Take-All E-commerce," *xconomy.com*, February 3, 2014, http://www.xconomy.com/boston/2014/02/03/2b-wayfair-valuation-a-big-statement-in-winner-take-all-e-commerce/

[12] Jeff Bertolucci, "Online Retailer Uses DNA Research To Connect With Customers," *InformationWeek.com*, September 24, 2012, http://www.informationweek.com/big-data/big-data-analytics/online-retailer-uses-dna-research-to-connect-with-customers/d/d-id/1106475.

[13] "Markov Chain," http://en.wikipedia.org/wiki/Markov_chain.

It then describes how Ben's team applied that technique to identify more meaningful connections among products that Wayfair's recommendation system could then consider in what it showed its customers. In the article, Ben estimated an increase of 18% in customer click-throughs after implementing the new recommendation algorithm. (Very generously, he had written two blog posts that describe the ideas in further detail.[14, 15])

As I listened to Ben and re-read his posts, what became clear was that while recommendation systems[16] have been around for a long time (for example, Amazon's collaborative filtering[17] features) and have been heavily promoted by commercial software vendors (for example, Oracle/Endeca's guided search tools), the widely varying nature of the underlying data from situation to situation makes it very difficult to generalize a recommendation algorithm. Past the most basic things, like "users who looked at/rented this also looked at/rented that," things get flaky. The algorithm that won the Netflix Prize, for doing the best job of suggesting movies you might like to see, is going to make those recommendations based on information with very different properties from what's available from observing browsers of home furnishing products. For example, while the concepts of "genre" and "director" might be analogous to "style" and "designer," films mostly lack properties that furnishings have, such as uses, or belonging to sets of complementary pieces. Similarly, the behavior markers and patterns of users on media sites versus shopping sites will also look very different.

[14] Ben Clark, "Recommendations with simple correlation metrics on implied preference data," *Wayfair Engineering* (blog), January 30, 2013, http://engineering.wayfair.com/recommendations-with-simple-correlation-metrics-on-implied-preference-data/.

[15] Ben Clark, "Recommendations With Markov Clustering," *Wayfair Engineering* (blog), February 23, 2012, http://engineering.wayfair.com/recommendations-with-markov-clustering/.

[16] "Recommender System," http://en.wikipedia.org/wiki/Recommender_system.

[17] "Collaborative Filtering," http://en.wikipedia.org/wiki/Collaborative_filtering.

Readers of *Pragmalytics* will guess that I was most interested in learning how Ben and his colleagues approach their work so that they don't quickly hit diminishing returns as they seek increasingly exotic ways to improve recommendations. So we talked further about Wayfair's approach to developing potentially useful algorithms. This extended to their development philosophy, the infrastructure and architecture choices they've made along the way, and to the skills they've assembled and how they've organized them.

To improve their recommendation algorithms, Ben and his colleagues blend a machine learning approach with close, iterative oversight from humans. "Any data scientist worth his salt will tell you that the projects that succeed are the ones where, if you're using machine learning, you've also got an oracle you can go to in order to vet results and narrow the problem to the point where machine processes can handle it. We do 'unsupervised' exercises like topic modeling,[18] but even on those we apply sanity checks by domain experts, like our merchandisers, who really understand not just what would pair well, but also why." Interestingly, while his team enriches its characterization of its shoppers with models from external services, they suspect that these models are slightly skewed toward an older, "less-Internet" population, and so Wayfair tends to weight its own data more heavily in developing its recommendation rules. Also notable is the silver lining Ben feels the batch processing nature of analytic jobs creates. He suggests that "batch is a buffer" that gives him and his team time to experiment with algorithms that in faster update cycles they might not have a chance to try.

Examples like these illustrate a strong ability and interest at the firm to "get under the hood." Ben memorably described how his former Digitas colleague and Hut 8 Labs co-founder Dan Milstein inspired him with the question, "What Would Han Solo Do?"

---

[18] "Topic Model," http://en.wikipedia.org/wiki/Topic_model.

Star Wars fans will recall the various descriptions of Solo's ship, the *Millennium Falcon*, as a mix of home brew and high performance.[19] In the software engineering world, the reference is a metaphor for talented engineers hacking on a shoestring budget to prove out their ideas, and then investing to automate fully only the winning ideas. There's a software equivalent, if you will, of getting yourself in motion, and even up to very high speed, by having a wookie bang on a cheap component with a wrench, possibly complaining the whole time that he needs a better, more expensive one. This contrasts strongly with a more conventional approach many retailers take of making big commitments to commercial application software, and then not taking advantage of most features (and sometimes, of none at all). "This is one of the things I and my team love about the ecommerce category," says Ben. "Margins are thin enough that they impose a discipline on you, and if you can work things out within the confines of that discipline, you can really beat the big guys at their own game. So we really take pride in the 'WWHSD' ethos here."

As for its analytic infrastructure, Wayfair runs things on a "modern but non-cloud" platform, with Hadoop handling a large amount of log file processing, and then a commercial MPP (massively parallel processing) database implementation alongside that for analysis and reporting. Ben observes that the choice of colocation rather than cloud is likely more a function of when Wayfair got going, noting that if you're just starting out today it is much easier and cheaper to provision your platform through an Amazon or Rackspace cloud than to buy, set up, and maintain all your own servers and software. He went on to note, however, that at Wayfair's current and projected scale, it's not just more economical to provision its own tools, but it also gives a higher degree of responsiveness and control—"If you need to tweak

---

[19] "Quotes About The Millennium Falcon," http://www.oocities.org/daala240/falcon.html.

virtual machines below the level of what a hypervisor[20] provides, for example," he says—that the cloud vendors don't match.

The technical team at Wayfair reflects both the firm's unique approach to creating value and the entrepreneurial spirit that has gotten it this far. "Because we run our own hardware, we're more weighted toward UNIX sysadmins (system administrators) than DBAs, at least compared to what you might otherwise find these days," he says. Working closely with this platform support team are two other groups: Ben's engineering team and a Business Intelligence team that's responsible for analysis and reporting. Ben's team is roughly half oriented toward application development (it includes members with advanced degrees in physics, aeronautics, and computer science) and half toward the data science that informs their application development efforts. The BI team is more heavily weighted toward data science ("more economics and statistics degrees there," says Ben) but includes former full-time programmers who now do the hands-on part of their work in R and SQL. Wayfair's CEO, Niraj Shah, famously commented on a panel during 2013 that half the members of the firm's marketing team knew SQL well enough to run their own database queries.

Wayfair's engineering team is all on-shore. Being in Boston, with its deep academic wells and a vibrant digital startup scene and venture-backed business ecosystem to draw from helps a great deal. But Ben notes that one of the biggest draws is how well the various technical groups collaborate with each other across what elsewhere might end up as silos. As the firm continues to grow and inevitably draws the gaze of current and future competitors (Amazon chief among them), it will need to continue to innovate furiously, and all these advantages will be brought to bear to make that happen.

---

[20] Software that allows operating system administrators to monitor and manage multiple virtual machines running on shared or cloud-based hardware. See "Hypervisor," http://en.wikipedia.org/wiki/Hypervisor.

Index

A

Abbott, 68
accelerating progress, 20
access to data, 29
    analytic maturity model, 35-37
    BENS BRN story, 38-40
    Big Data investments, 40-44
    ceno-analytic era, 32-33
    data warehouses, 37
    defining requirements, 44-46
    external source management, 46-48
    future of, 34-35
    meso-analytic era, 31
    modern times, 33-34
    obtaining data, 29-40
    paleo-analytic era, 29-30
accountability, 125
    effectiveness, 127
    usage of resources, 134
acquisitions, eCPA (effective Cost Per Acquisition), 97
Acxiom, 158
adding variables, 20

ad hoc approaches to
    defining data requirements, 44-46
    exploration by analysts, 133
Adobe Test & Target, 171
Adometry, 84
Aetna Insurance, 28, 61. *See also* Lang, Belinda
algorithms, recommendation, 221
alignment
    optimization, 84
    strategic, 13-14
Amazon, 171, 223
American Express, 28, 69, 166, 177, 200
analysis
    attribution, 97-99, 150
    Bayesian, 118
    biases, 119. *See also bias*
    cohort, 184
    Common Requirements Frameworks, 54
    forensic, 157
    Google Analytics, 53
    orchestrating, 27
    skills, 64

Experian, 158, 161
external conditions, forcing
change, 137
external source management, 46-48

F

Falcon, 222
fault lines, organizational, 23-26
feasibility, assessments, 105
feedback, loops, 20
file sizes, 157. *See also* digital
revolution
flexibility. *See* operational flexibility
flowcharts, 17
focus, framing beyond answers, 14-15
Forbes, 77
Force Five Partners, 126, 128
forensic analysis, 157
formulas for change, 137-140
Fort Point Partners, 171
frameworks, 73
Analytic Brief, 73-87
Common Requirements
Frameworks, 50-56
Customer Decision Journey, 77
Service Profit Chain, 170
Frank, Annemarie, 97
conversations, 177-181
frequency, Recent, Frequency, and
Monetary Value (RFM), 51
frosting, 157
Fuller, Joe, 147
funnels, 74
future of access to data, 34-35

G

Gartner, 113
gathering data, 90. *See also* research
geo-target advertising
investments, 103

Glamour, 154. *See also* Condé Nast
Glengarry Glen Ross, 23
Global Marketing Council, 146
Google Analytics, 53
Google Display Network, 53
Google Trends, 103
governance
models, 133-136
processes, 46
grading customers Recent, 51
grids, Purchase Process chart, 78
gross margins, 51
GSI Commerce, 171

H

Hadoop, 40-41, 67, 193
Harrah's, 61-62, 65
Hartford, The, 126. *See also*
Purcell, Todd
Harvard Business Review, 32
Harvard Business School, 147
Harvard University, 210-213
harvesting results, 128-131
heat maps, Purchase Process chart, 78
Hewitt, Perry, 190
conversations, 210-213
historical models
ceno-analytic era, 32-33
data access, 29-40
future of access to data, 34-35
meso-analytic era, 31
modern times, 33-34
paleo-analytic era, 29-30
home office vs. the field tension, 24
Honig, Judy, 199
Howe, Peter J., 38
HSN, 97, 177-181. *See also* Frank,
Annemarie
Hsu, Jeremy, 20